Human Papillomavirus (HPV)

Titles in the Diseases and Disorders series include:

Acne
AIDS
Alzheimer's Disease
Anorexia and Bulimia
Anthrax
Arthritis
Attention Deficit Disorder
Autism
Bipolar Disorder
Birth Defects
Brain Tumors
Breast Cancer
Cerebral Palsy
Chronic Fatigue
   Syndrome
Cystic Fibrosis
Deafness
Diabetes
Down Syndrome
Dyslexia
The Ebola Virus
Epilepsy
Fetal Alcohol Syndrome
Flu
Food Poisoning
Growth Disorders
Headaches
Heart Disease

Hemophilia
Hepatitis
Leukemia
Lou Gehrig's Disease
Lyme Disease
Mad Cow Disease
Malaria
Malnutrition
Measles and Rubella
Meningitis
Mental Retardation
Multiple Sclerosis
Obesity
Ovarian Cancer
Parkinson's Disease
Phobias
Prostate Cancer
SARS
Schizophrenia
Sexually Transmitted
   Diseases
Sleep Disorders
Smallpox
Strokes
Teen Depression
Toxic Shock Syndrome
Tuberculosis
West Nile Virus

Human Papillomavirus (HPV)

Don Nardo

LUCENT BOOKS

An imprint of Thomson Gale, a part of The Thomson Corporation

THOMSON

GALE

™

Detroit • New York • San Francisco • New Haven, Conn. • Waterville, Maine • London

LIBRARY OF CONGRESS CATALOGING-IN-PUBLICATION DATA

Nardo, Don, 1947-
    Human papillomavirus (HPV) / by Don Nardo.
        p. cm. — (Diseases and disorders)
    Includes bibliographical references and index.
    ISBN-13: 978-1-59018-998-6 (hardcover)
    1. Papillomaviruses--Juvenile literature. I. Title.
QR406.N37 2007
616.9'11—dc22

                                                    2007015827

ISBN-10: 1-59018-998-1

Printed in the United States of America

Table of Contents

"The Most Difficult Puzzles Ever Devised"

Charles Best, one of the pioneers in the search for a cure for diabetes, once explained what it is about medical research that intrigued him so. "It's not just the gratification of knowing one is helping people," he confided, "although that probably is a more heroic and selfless motivation. Those feelings may enter in, but truly, what I find best is the feeling of going toe to toe with nature, of trying to solve the most difficult puzzles ever devised. The answers are there somewhere, those keys that will solve the puzzle and make the patient well. But how will those keys be found?"

Since the dawn of civilization, nothing has so puzzled people—and often frightened them, as well—as the onset of illness in a body or mind that had seemed healthy before. A seizure, the inability of a heart to pump, the sudden deterioration of muscle tone in a small child—being unable to reverse such conditions or even to understand why they occur was unspeakably frustrating to healers. Even before there were names for such conditions, even before they were understood at all, each was a reminder of how complex the human body was, and how vulnerable.

While our grappling with understanding diseases has been frustrating at times, it has also provided some of humankind's most heroic accomplishments. Alexander Fleming's accidental discovery in 1928 of a mold that could be turned into penicillin has resulted in the saving of untold millions of lives. The isolation of the enzyme insulin has reversed what was once a death sentence for anyone with diabetes. There have been great strides in combating conditions for which there is not yet a cure, too. Medicines can help AIDS patients live longer, diagnostic tools such as mammography and ultrasounds can help doctors find tumors while they are treatable, and laser surgery techniques have made the most intricate, minute operations routine.

This "toe-to-toe" competition with diseases and disorders is even more remarkable when seen in a historical continuum. An astonishing amount of progress has been made in a very short time. Just two hundred years ago, the existence of germs as a cause of some diseases was unknown. In fact, it was less than 150 years ago that a British surgeon named Joseph Lister had difficulty persuading his fellow doctors that washing their hands before delivering a baby might increase the chances of a healthy delivery (especially if they had just attended to a diseased patient)!

Each book in Lucent's Diseases and Disorders series explores a disease or disorder and the knowledge that has been accumulated (or discarded) by doctors through the years. Each book also examines the tools used for pinpointing a diagnosis, as well as the various means that are used to treat or cure a disease. Finally, new ideas are presented—techniques or medicines that may be on the horizon.

Frustration and disappointment are still part of medicine, for not every disease or condition can be cured or prevented. But the limitations of knowledge are being pushed outward constantly; the "most difficult puzzles ever devised" are finding challengers every day.

The STD Most People Never Heard Of

Almost everyone has heard of the sexually transmitted diseases (STDs) gonorrhea and syphilis. And practically everybody knows that HIV is the virus, sometimes transmitted sexually, that can cause the serious disease AIDS. Likewise, a majority of Americans are aware of the existence of another common STD, herpes. They have heard that herpes can cause recurring outbreaks of cold sore–like blisters in the genital areas of both men and women.

These diseases are certainly prevalent, infectious, and should be taken seriously and guarded against. Yet none of them are nearly as widespread in societies across the world as the human papillomavirus, most often called HPV for short. In fact, HPV is so prevalent that at least 75 percent of sexually active men and women come into contact with it at some time in their lives.

Although HPV is routinely referred to as "the HPV virus," it is not a single virus. Rather, it is a group of more than a hundred related viruses that infect the skin, often (but certainly not always) around the genitals. In many cases the HPV disappears on its own after a few months or a year or so. But while a person carries it, he or she can pass it on to one or more sexual partners, some of whom will become infected. At least 20 million people in the United States, or nearly 7 percent of the

population, are presently infected with HPV. Some of these people have or will eventually develop small, harmless warts on their feet, legs, hands, or faces. Others will develop diseases such as genital warts, cervical cancer (or cancer of the cervix), or other kinds of cancer.

"Human Papilloma What?"

Considering how widespread HPV is, one would assume that, like gonorrhea, HIV, and herpes, it would be well known among the general population. And yet this is not the case. Indeed, HPV remains one of the least-known STDs that plague human society. As noted physician and research scientist Gregory S. Henderson quips: "When I meet a patient newly diagnosed with HPV, the first reaction is usually a blank stare, followed by the inevitable question, 'Human papilloma what?'"[1]

The consequences of public ignorance of any serious disease and its symptoms (physical signs) can be unfortunate and in some cases fatal. And HPV has been no exception. Henderson tells the story of "Kate," one of his patients. Once a healthy,

HPV causes small, harmless warts like the one seen here, as well as the more serious genital warts.

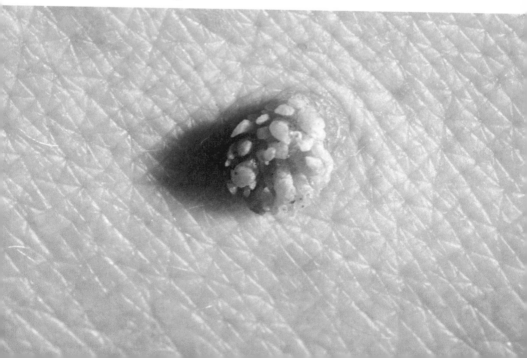

vibrant young woman, she contracted HPV perhaps in her late teens or early twenties. Eventually, she developed cervical cancer and died at age thirty-two. "After being diagnosed," Henderson writes,

> Kate's first response was typical: "Why me?". . . . She really wanted to understand how she had contracted this disease. In the course of her explorations, she spoke to an old high school classmate who . . . was also suffering from invasive cervical cancer. Kate began to understand that she and her friend had probably both contracted HPV from the same boy. Now, ten years later, she was paying the price of not knowing that the virus exists, what impact it can have . . . and how to prevent its devastating consequences. She was pained and baffled by the lack of information. "Why didn't someone tell us about this illness?" she asked.[2]

Henderson goes on to explain that he has treated hundreds of women who, like Kate, developed serious complications of HPV. And none of them had ever heard of the virus. Moreover, Henderson questioned medical colleagues across the country, and their experiences were virtually the same. "Few patients had ever heard of HPV, and none knew about its connection to cervical cancer."[3]

Old but Not Well Understood

These disturbing facts naturally raise the question of why so little is known about HPV by the general public. Part of the answer is a considerable lack of understanding of the virus within the general medical community until relatively recently. This does not mean that HPV is a new phenomenon. In fact, evidence shows that it and the serious conditions it causes have existed throughout human history. The ancient Greeks recognized the existence of genital warts, for instance. The second-century A.D. Greek physician Soranus even wrote a treatise titled *On Warty Growths of the Female Genitals*. Soranus and his colleagues also recognized that such warts could pass from one person to another during sexual relations.

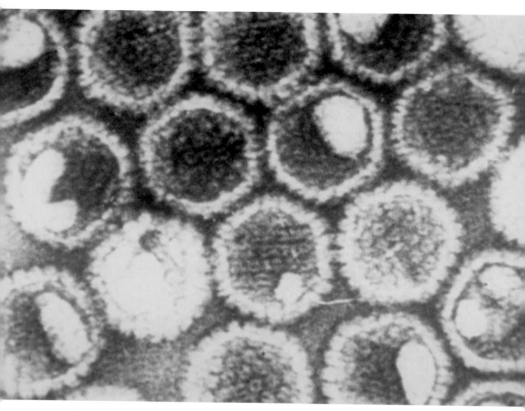

Cervical cancer was originally thought to have been caused by the herpes simplex virus (HSV) until the early 1990s, when the link between HPV and cervical cancer was firmly established.

However, they did not understand why, since the germ theory of disease would not be introduced until some sixteen centuries later. They also did not realize that genital warts and ordinary warts on other areas of the body are related.

Even after the discovery in the 1800s that germs (bacteria and viruses) cause disease, doctors were slow to understand HPV and its role in cervical cancer and other diseases. Indeed, as late as the early 1980s the vast majority of physicians and researchers thought that cervical cancer was caused mainly by the herpes simplex virus (HSV). Only in the early 1990s was the link between HPV and cervical cancer established beyond the shadow of a doubt.

Thus, firmly reliable information about HPV and its consequences did not exist until relatively recently. And one result may have been a failure among many doctors to educate themselves and the general public about the virus. Professor of medicine Joel Palefsky of the University of California–San Francisco, points out:

> A few doctors don't know much about HPV themselves. Maybe they don't even know the risks involved with HPV. Others don't bother saying anything about HPV because there's no treatment for the virus itself, only treatment of the diseases the virus causes. . . . They're all reasons why you may have to bring up the subject with your doctor if he or she doesn't.[4]

Still another reason why so few people are familiar with HPV is that the infections it causes can and often do show few or no symptoms. In such cases, only later, when warts or cancer develop, do clear-cut symptoms appear. This makes HPV easy to miss and allows it to remain hidden and ready to strike unsuspecting victims. Only when large numbers of people are equipped with the facts about this silent threat can society begin to eradicate it or at least significantly reduce the number of people it victimizes.

Finding Reliable Facts About HPV

That little or nothing was known about the human papillomavirus, or HPV, before the 1980s makes it one of the least understood viruses that affect the human community on a large scale. For that reason, the medical and popular literature about HPV remains relatively scant. In comparison, a great deal more has been written about HIV, herpes, avian flu, and other viruses that threaten the general population.

Moreover, even much of what was written about HPV in the past few decades is now sorely out of date and therefore unreliable. As the American Social Health Association (ASHA) reports:

> New information about HPV has been learned in recent years, reversing some previous assumptions about the virus. The result is that older publications may be inaccurate, when they mention HPV at all. Likewise, health care professionals, writers, and educators who have not kept up with recent research findings may continue to spread misconceptions. Another difficulty is that to some degree, the overall topic of genital HPV is complex and confusing to everyone, lay person and scientist alike.[5]

Thus, a large amount of incorrect information has been perpetuated both in writing and by word of mouth about HPV and

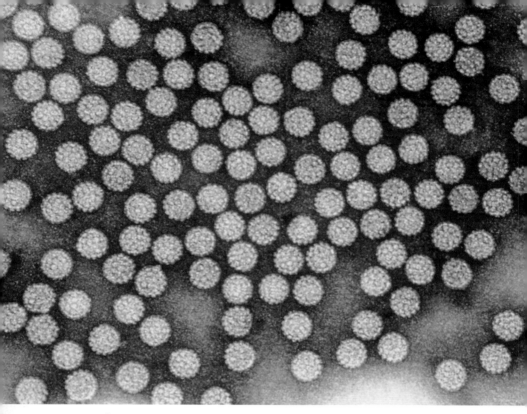

HPV cells, as seen under a microscope. HPV is one of the least understood viruses affecting the human community.

its consequences. As a result, a number of myths have arisen about the subject, particularly about which people are more likely to contract HPV and how the infection spreads.

Far from Rare

One of the more prevalent of these myths is sometimes called the "I'm the only one" assumption. Most often, a person who discovers that he or she has contracted HPV has never heard of it prior to that moment. And the person assumes that if the virus was common, he or she would surely have heard people talk about it before. At one time or another, for instance, nearly everybody has heard others mention or talk about HIV (or AIDs, which HIV can lead to) or gonorrhea. Therefore, the person reasons, an HPV infection must be very rare. And he or she has had the misfortune to catch a disease that medical science does not understand well and may not be able to treat. Not surprisingly, this assumption can cause a great deal of anxiety.

"I was terrified after my doctor told me I had it," says Karen, who contracted HPV in 2006.

> He didn't mention how common it was . . . only that I must have gotten it from sex. I never heard anybody mention it before, so I figured very few people got it, which could mean there's either no really effective treatment for it or else I might end up as some kind of guinea pig while the doctors experimented with new treatments and stuff. Until I went out and read up on HPV for myself, I was . . . [such] a nervous wreck that I had trouble sleeping.[6]

In reality, however, the reason that Karen and others like her have not heard people talk about HPV before is that so few

Actress Elisabeth Rohm films a public service announcement to raise awareness of the link between cervical cancer and HPV.

people know anything about it. And even those few who do know something about the virus are, more likely than not, reluctant to talk about it. "Those struggling with this troubling condition or strange new diagnosis rarely discuss it with others," ASHA points out,

> since it would seem unlikely that they would understand. And others—your second-best friend, your cousin, your coworker, your neighbor across the street—likewise feel constrained to keep silent about their HPV, thinking that you wouldn't understand. The net result is that very few

Do Condoms Protect Against HPV?

The answer to the above question is "a little, but often not enough." True, condoms can be very—though not 100 percent— effective against certain STDs, particularly gonorrhea and HIV, which spread via bodily fluids. This is because a condom, when properly used, captures all, or at least most, of the fluids involved. In contrast, HPV spreads through skin-to-skin contact. And as the American Social Health Association explains:

Condoms do not cover the entire genital area of either sex. They leave the vulva, anus, perineal area [between the anus and vagina in women and between the anus and scrotum in men], base of the penis, and scrotum uncovered, and contact between these areas can transmit HPV. . . . That is not to say condoms are useless. In fact, studies have shown condom use can lower the risk of acquiring HPV infection and reduce the risk of HPV-related diseases, as well as help prevent other STDs and unintended pregnancy.

American Social Health Association, "HPV: Myths and Misconceptions." www.ashastd. org/hpv/hpv_learn_myths.cfm.

people ever have the chance to place genital HPV in an accurate context, as the very common virus it really is.[7]

Indeed, HPV is far from rare. On the one hand, the Centers for Disease Control and Prevention (CDC) reports, roughly 20 million people in the United States are infected with HPV at any given moment. Moreover, approximately 50 percent of sexually active men and women in the country will contract the infection at some point in their lives. (Although men are just as likely as women to carry HPV, for reasons that are not well understood far fewer men than women develop cancer from the virus. For this reason, HPV is sometimes called a woman's disease, when in fact it can and does affect both sexes.) Also, some 80 percent of women older than age fifty will acquire an HPV infection at one time or another. And more than 6 million Americans are newly infected with HPV each year. Thus, any person who is diagnosed with an HPV infection need not fear that they are alone.

Granted, the CDC and other authorities on STDs caution that a majority of those who do become infected with HPV remain so only briefly—a few months to a year or two. However, a significant number remain infected longer. And of these, some develop unpleasant or dangerous physical ailments.

How HPV Invades the Body

Another common myth about HPV relates to its mode of transmission, or the manner in which it spreads. Because the virus is so often classified as an STD, a frequent assumption is that it spreads only through intimate sexual contact. Or put another way, only people who have sexual intercourse can get HPV.

But the reality is often quite different. It is true that some versions of the HPV virus specifically target the genital area. But the majority of HPV viruses do not. For example, some cause ordinary warts, including plantar warts on the feet, and do not usually spread through sexual contact. In general, infection by HPV occurs through the skin, via skin-to-skin contact, most often from one person's skin to another person's skin. More important, the point of contact in which the infection occurs does not have to be in the genital area (although it

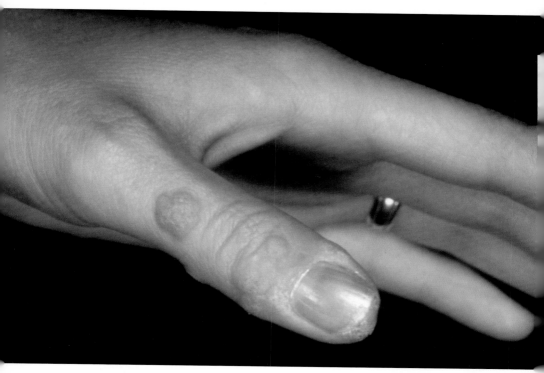

The HPV virus can spread to other parts of the body. For example, a wart on a finger or thumb can spread to adjacent fingers when these areas are touched by the virus.

quite often is). Any exposed patch of skin is vulnerable to one version or another of the virus.

To understand how the HPV virus actually invades the skin requires some basic knowledge of what viruses are and how they operate. Viruses are the smallest of the many different kinds of germs, including bacteria, protozoa, and others. In fact, an average virus is thousands of times smaller than an average bacterium, which is itself microscopic. This means that viruses are visible only under very powerful microscopes. These tiny germs are essentially thin, twisted strands with a surprisingly simple makeup. Each consists of a bit of protein and a touch of a chemical called nucleic acid.

Unlike most other types of germs, viruses cannot reproduce on their own, in a pond for instance, or on a rock, or in a lab

dish. Viruses can reproduce only inside the cells of living organisms (plants or animals), which makes these germs true parasites. Once a virus has invaded a host cell it can, through reproduction, spread to and take up residence in nearby cells. In this way a viral disease can steadily spread through a host plant or animal.

In the case of HPV, the virus is particularly tough and hardy. It can live for an undetermined length of time—at least several hours and perhaps several days—on the skin's surface (though it cannot reproduce outside of a cell). Millions of viruses can attach themselves to a single outer skin cell, called a squamous cell.

The Virus Spreads

Ideally, however, in order to reproduce quickly and easily and establish an infection, these viruses need to reach the cells in the lower layer of the skin. Called the basal cells, these are constantly dividing and creating fresh skin cells. The HPV viral strands can reach the basal cells by entering tiny tears or abrasions in the outer layers of the skin. People acquire these microinjuries regularly, simply by bumping into or rubbing up against ordinary objects. Such injuries are usually too small to see or feel and they heal within minutes or hours. But before they heal they offer an opening to invading HPV germs. Meanwhile, the HPV virus can even more easily invade the body by settling in the moist mucous membranes inside the mouth, throat, nose, vagina, penis, and rectum.

Having made an initial inroad into the cells of a host body, the HPV virus can, under the right circumstances, spread to other parts of that body. Thus, if one develops a wart on one's finger, the HPV viruses in the wart can easily spread to adjacent fingers when the fingers touch. Similarly, touching a plantar wart on the foot can spread the virus to the fingers or other parts of the body. Also, some HPV viruses can establish themselves in the genital area. And a person (A) can pass these germs on to his or her partner (B) simply by touching, either by A's genital area contacting B's genital area directly, or by a finger first touching A's genital area and then touching B's. This

means that a genital HPV infection can occur even when full or partial sexual intercourse does not occur.

In fact, HPV viruses are so hardy and can spread so readily that doctors must take special precautions when operating on HPV-infected patients. One example, described here by Henderson, is removal of genital warts by a laser:

> During this procedure, surgeons and operating room staff must wear a special ultra-filter mask because even in the vapor that is generated from the lasered warts, infective viruses can survive and enter the nasal passages and upper respiratory tracts. They can take up residence in the nose, mouth, throat, and respiratory tract, causing warty lesions [sores] in these areas too.[8]

Dormant or Active?

The peculiar ways that HPV viruses behave once they have invaded the human body have given rise to another common myth about HPV. Namely, if someone in a monogamous relationship (one confined to two people) is diagnosed with an HPV-related disease, it means that one of the partners has cheated. This misconception is based partly on the mistaken idea that the virus is contracted only through intimate sexual contact. The fact is that it could also have been passed along unknowingly through casual skin-to-skin contact in a school, office, or other public setting.

The cheating myth is also based on the notion that the HPV virus always leads to the development of warts, cancer, or some other serious condition very soon after entering the body. This does happen in a minority of cases. But far more often the virus, having entered the body, stays dormant, or in a sense lays low. It can remain more or less inactive and undetected for several months or even a few years. Thus, even if the HPV did enter the body through sexual contact, the infection may well have occurred long before the beginning of the monogamous relationship in question. "My husband was relieved when he learned how you can have HPV in your body for a long time," says Mary, whose HPV infection led to an out-

HPV Throat Infections

Laryngeal papillomatosis (also referred to as recurrent respiratory papillomatosis) is the development of HPV-related growths or tumors in the throat, most often the larynx, or voice box. It remains uncertain how many people are affected by this condition. But medical authorities estimate that between 60 and 80 percent of the cases involve children under the age of three. The rest are older children and adults. Many of the victims contract HPV during the birth process because their mothers are infected by HPV. Laryngeal papillomatosis causes difficulty in breathing, swallowing, and/or sleeping. Affected adults also experience frequent coughing or hoarseness. To treat the condition, doctors sometimes remove the growths using traditional surgery. Increasingly, however, laser surgery—using a carbon dioxide laser—is also being employed. Unfortunately, even after surgery the growths can grow back, requiring the patient to undergo additional surgeries. In extreme cases, doctors perform a tracheotomy (make an incision in the throat) and insert a small tube to help the patient breathe.

break of genital warts. "It's not that he didn't believe me when I told him I'd never been with anyone else. But I think he had, you know, kind of a suspicion about it, which I guess is pretty understandable. Our doctor explained how I could've caught the HPV before we met."[9]

It is also worth noting another possibility in Mary's case. Her husband could have slept with someone else who was infected with HPV. As a carrier, the husband could have passed the virus on to Mary, who then developed genital warts.

Physicians and scientists do not yet completely understand why HPV quickly becomes active in some people and remains long dormant in others. One reason may be differences among the hundred-plus HPV viruses themselves. "HPVs aren't all alike," Palefsky points out.

"Some are more aggressive than others. Scientists have also learned recently that even among a given HPV type . . . some variants of it are worse than others. So here we have a luck of the draw—if you're exposed to HPV, you hope that it'll be a . . . low-risk [kind]."[10]

Other factors determining the speed and severity of an HPV attack could be the genetic background, everyday behaviors, and mental outlook of the infected person. Some people have so-called "good genes." This means that, in part because of their genetic makeup, their parents and grandparents tended to have low risks of catching various diseases (and often lived longer than average). The infected person may have inherited

Smoking increases a woman's risk of developing HPV complications, such as genital warts or cervical cancer.

these good genes. If so, he or she may have a low risk of contracting cancer despite the presence of HPV in his or her body. Also, behaviors such as smoking and poor diet are known to increase the likelihood of developing cancer and other diseases, as is persistent mental stress. Thus, it may be that people who have favorable genetic backgrounds, eat nutritious foods, do not smoke, and experience little stress are much less likely to experience serious complications of the HPV virus.

From Low to High Risk

Therefore, the consequences of contracting the HPV virus can be very minor for some people and more serious, or even severe, for others. Those tens of millions of people who are fortunate enough to have minor consequences will experience what medical expert Lynda Rushing calls "the disappearing virus." Doctors are "beginning to understand the natural history of this virus," she says.

> It appears that HPV infection in most women is a short-lived infection that produces no [cancer-related consequences]. After initial exposure during sex, it takes somewhere between 6 weeks and 6 months for the virus to be detected in a woman. For most women, the virus is no longer detectable in 12 to 18 months.[11]

In such cases, for reasons still not well understood, the woman's body rids itself of HPV. On occasion the virus will remain in the body longer than eighteen months. In such a situation it will either remain dormant and eventually disappear or remain dormant indefinitely. HPV also disappears from most men's bodies over the course of time.

For a much smaller number of women and men, the HPV virus remains in the body and leads to consequences ranging from uncomfortable to, in a few cases, lethal. For example, about a million people (or almost 1 percent of the adult population) in the United States—including both women and men—develop genital warts each year. Several million others develop other kinds of warts, such as plantar warts on the soles of the feet. And roughly 10,000 to 12,000 women develop cervical

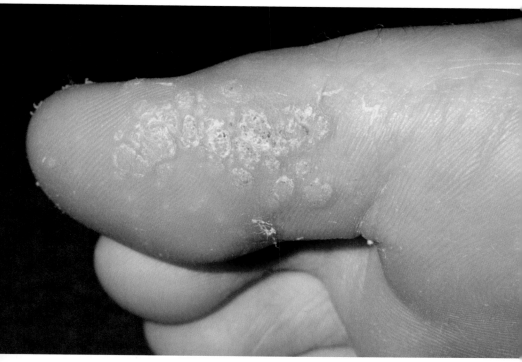

Plantar warts are shown here on a patient's big toe.

cancer caused by HPV. Of these, more than 4,000 die. In addition, a few thousand people with HPV go on to develop other
cancers, including anal cancer, cancer of the penis, cancer of
the mouth, head and neck cancers, and others.

Each of these unpleasant consequences of HPV is caused by
a different version (sometimes called a strain) of the virus.
Medical experts have designated each version with a number.
Thus, HPV version or strain 1 is associated with plantar warts.
HPV 2, 6, 11, and 16 are known to cause genital warts, while
oral cancers are associated with HPV 16, 18, 36, and 57. A number of HPV strains are sometimes called "high risk" because
they can lead to cervical, penile, anal, and other cancers. These
strains include HPV 16, 18, 31, 33, 35, 45, 51, 52, 59, and 68,
among others. In contrast, HPV 42, 43, 44, and a few others are
considered "low risk" because they usually do not result in un-
savory consequences.

Another HPV tragedy results when a woman with genital warts passes on her infection to her infant during the birth process. Fortunately, this situation, which is associated only with HPV 6 and 11, is rare. When it does occur, the child is infected with the virus as it passes through the birth canal. He or she soon develops sores on the vocal cords, a condition known as laryngeal papillomatosis. This condition is treatable through laser surgery.

Consequences for Society

Society as a whole is affected when people infected by or carrying HPV pass it on to others. This happens millions of times a year in the United States alone, almost always unbeknownst to the people involved. Though a majority of those who pick up the virus this way each year will not suffer serious consequences, tens of thousands will. And a few thousand of them will die of cancer.

The monetary costs of HPV for society are also great. More than $5 billion is spent in the United States each year to screen for cervical cancer. And treating HPV infections costs close to $2 billion. There are also the large hidden and uncalculated costs of millions of lost work hours for those who go to doctors or hospitals for testing or treatment. Whether directly or indirectly, HPV affects nearly everyone in society, more often than not in unwanted ways.

CHAPTER TWO

Screening for and Diagnosing HPV

With most diseases and medical conditions, the first line of defense for the victim is noticing and recognizing one or more classic symptoms, or physical signs. The flu, for example, almost always displays symptoms such as fever, headache, runny nose, and sore throat. And typical symptoms of mononucleosis (or "mono") are fever, swollen glands in the throat, and extreme tiredness. Having observed these symptoms, a physician may administer various tests (a direct physical exam or laboratory analyses or both). These help him or her to achieve a diagnosis, or conclusive identification of the disease or condition.

The problem with the HPV virus is that at first it presents no obvious symptoms in the vast majority of people it infects. On occasion, small warts or lesions (sores) might appear on or around the vagina, anus, penis, hands, foot, mouth, or other infected area soon after infection occurs. But this is usually not the case.

In the vast majority of cases of HPV in humans, one of two things happens. In the first and most common scenario, the virus remains dormant and hidden and eventually disappears. In the less common but more dangerous scenario, over time the virus causes cells in the infected area to become abnormal in various ways. These abnormal cells are sometimes labeled "precancerous" because they can later (though do not always)

26

develop into some form of cancer. Unfortunately for the infected individual, such abnormalities are not usually accompanied by noticeable symptoms. In most cases the infected area does not swell, change color, or itch. So the person may not realize that he or she has cancer until it is too late.

To guard against this unwanted outcome, doctors and medical researchers have developed some highly effective screening tests. A screening test is not a specific diagnostic test, but rather a first step in the diagnostic process. "The purpose of a screening test," Henderson explains,

> is to survey a very large at-risk population and narrow down the individuals who may be suffering from the disease or condition being investigated. Once the screening test has highlighted people with a possible problem, diagnostic tests can determine whether an actual problem is there, and if so, what it is. . . . In other words, the goal of a screening test is to avoid subjecting a very large group of people to diagnostic tests, which can often be more invasive, uncomfortable, and expensive.[12]

The Pap Smear—A Medical Mousetrap

By far the most common screening test for HPV and possible HPV-related cancers is the Pap smear. It is named after the physician who introduced it in 1949, George Papanicolaou. Though not perfect, on the whole it is an extremely effective and reliable test. "I consider the Pap test the mousetrap of diagnostic medicine," says Henderson, "because it is so effective, yet so simple in design. In fact, it's so simple it's amazing that no one came up with it before 1949."[13] Indeed, before the introduction of Pap smears, about 27 of every 100,000 women in the United States died of cervical cancer each year. Today, only 8 of every 100,000 women do so. That represents a reduction of almost 75 percent in the cervical cancer death rate, a truly significant positive development.

The general purpose of a Pap smear is to detect HPV-related abnormalities in the cells in a person's skin. In particular, a Pap smear can flag the presence of a precancerous condition. But

The Pap Smear's Namesake

The inventor of the Pap smear, George N. Papanicolaou, was a Greek American pathologist. Born on the Greek island of Euboea in 1883, he earned a medical degree in Athens in 1904 and moved with his wife to the United States in 1913. Papanicolaou became a U.S. citizen in 1927. In the years that followed he earned widespread recognition for his studies of the human reproductive tract at New York Hospital and Cornell Medical College. His most famous achievement was his screening test for cervical cancer. He first conceived it and described it to fellow doctors in the 1920s, but there was little interest in the medical community at the time. The situation changed, however, after he discussed the concept in his groundbreaking 1943 book, *Diagnosis of Uterine Cancer by the Vaginal Smear*. The idea of the Pap smear, named for him, then rapidly caught on with other American doctors. And by the 1950s the use of Pap smears was widespread in the United States and several other countries. Papanicolaou died in 1962. In 1978 the U.S. government honored his memory by publishing a stamp bearing his portrait.

George Papanicolaou invented the Pap smear.

A lab technician studies a Pap smear sample.

it can also show simply that an active HPV infection is present. A Pap smear is almost always administered to women in the area of the cervix, located inside the vagina. However, the same basic procedure can be and is occasionally done in the anal area of both women and men who are at high risk for developing abnormal cells in that area.

The National Cancer Institute reports that about 55 million Pap tests are performed each year on women in the United States. And of these, about 3.5 million, or roughly 6 percent, detect some kind of abnormal cells and lead to further tests.

The 55 million tests are performed on women in a wide age range. Government medical authorities advise women to have their first Pap smear no later than three years after having sexual intercourse for the first time (and/or no later than age twenty-one). After that, Pap smears are recommended every year until age thirty. At that point, if a woman's smears have all been negative, her doctor may advise her that she can begin having them every two to three years. After age sixty-five or

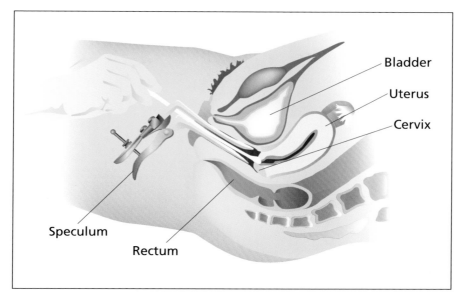

Bladder

Uterus

Cervix

Speculum

Rectum

This illustration shows the instruments used in a pelvic exam.

seventy, if previous Pap tests have been negative and her doctor approves, a woman may elect to discontinue the procedure.

In most cases, a woman having a Pap test lies on her back
on an examination table. The doctor then carefully inserts a
speculum, a metal or plastic device that spreads and holds
open the vaginal walls. This allows the doctor to see and reach
the cervix, the narrow opening of the lower uterus. The doctor
then gently scrapes the cervix's surface using a small spatula-
like instrument. Using an equally small brush, he or she brushes
the loosened cells onto a glass slide.

Interpreting Pap Smears

Following the collection of the Pap smear, the slide bearing the
cells is taken to a lab for analysis. The first step in the lab is to
stain the slide with liquids appropriately called Papanicolaou
stains. These make it easier to see the various parts of each cell,
especially the nucleus, or center. The technician, known as a
cytotechnologist, then places the slide under a microscope and
examines the cells. He or she is trained to recognize normal,
healthy cells as well as various abnormalities in cells.

Most often—at least 90 percent of the time—the cytotechnologist sees no abnormalities in the sample cells. These samples are therefore labeled "negative," meaning normal. But when any abnormal-looking cells are evident on the slide, he or she uses an ink pen to make a tiny dot next to each suspect cell. In most labs, as a precaution, a second cytotechnologist reviews 10 percent of the Pap smears labeled "negative" by the first one. If any mistakes were made in the first examination, the review usually catches them.

The slide with the questionable cells next goes to a pathologist, a doctor who is an expert at recognizing changes and abnormalities in cells, tissues, and organs. The pathologist confirms that the cells the cytotechnologist pinpointed are indeed abnormal. But how abnormal are they? Or more accurately, what is their degree and kind of abnormality? To clarify the degree and kind of abnormality in the cells, the pathologist usually classifies them using terms developed in the late 1980s and early 1990s for interpreting Pap smears. These terms are part of the Bethesda Classification System, first created in 1988 and later revised several times, most recently in 2001.

Classification Levels

The least harmful and worrisome level on the Pap test classification scale is the "low-grade squamous intraepithelial lesion," abbreviated LSIL (or LGSIL). Essentially, LSIL indicates a mild form of dysplasia. Dysplasia is an area of abnormal cells caused by an HPV infection. Thus, LSIL and mild dysplasia are two different ways of saying that the patient is infected with HPV but the infection is in an early stage and not yet precancerous. The most common approach in such cases is "watch and wait." That is, the doctor orders further Pap smears over the next several months, and these are carefully evaluated. It is hoped that during this period the body's immune system will get rid of the HPV on its own. In a minority of cases of LSIL, the doctor recommends surgical removal of the lesion as a precaution. In such cases, further Pap smears are taken to make sure that no abnormal cells have returned.

A more worrisome level in the Pap smear classification scale is the "high-grade squamous intraepithelial lesion," abbreviated HSIL (or HGSIL). HSIL indicates moderate or severe dysplasia, a precancerous condition. According to the National Cancer Institute, "there are more marked changes in the size and shape of the abnormal (precancerous) cells, meaning that the cells look very different from normal cells. HSILs are more severe abnormalities [than LSILs] and have a higher likelihood of progressing to invasive cancer."[14] In cases in which a Pap test indicates moderate or severe dysplasia, the lesion is always surgically removed.

Sometimes Pap smears produce results that do not fall into the negative, LSIL, or HSIL categories. The pathologist sees clearly that the cells under examination are abnormal but is unsure if they are HPV-related, precancerous, or perhaps something else. Such questionable sample cells are usually labeled "atypical squamous cells of undetermined significance," or ASCUS. An ASCUS lesion or abnormality might indeed be caused by HPV. But it can have several other causes, including hormonal changes in the body, side effects of certain medications, and even a deficiency of the B vitamin folic acid in the diet. To determine the real cause of ASCUS, doctors usually move on to the next steps in the diagnostic process.

Colposcopy and Biopsy

When the lab results indicate either HSIL or ASCUS, it is necessary to achieve a definite diagnosis of the stage of the HPV infection. This will guide the doctor in treating the patient. The next standard steps in diagnosing HPV are called colposcopy and biopsy. A colposcopy involves an instrument called a colposcope, which is a special portable microscope equipped with a very bright light. The patient lies on her back, just as she did for her Pap smear. This time, the doctor first coats the cervix with a solution of vinegar and iodine to make any lesions present more visible. Then he or she carefully inserts the colposcope and by peering into it closely examines the tissues of the cervix.

If the colposcopy reveals any lesions, even very small ones, the doctor next performs a biopsy. A biopsy is the removal of a

small piece of tissue from an area of the body under examination, in this case the cervix. The excised tissue is placed on a slide and given to a pathologist to examine.

The benefit of obtaining such a sample is that it includes cells from the base of the cervical tissue as well as its surface, giving a much fuller picture of the infected area. Rushing compares the diagnostic abilities of Pap smears and biopsies to bricks and brick walls. Scraping cells from the surface of cervix, she says, is like

> finding a few bricks scattered around an empty lot. We can guess that a house likely was once present on that lot, but our suspicions are confirmed when we find intact portions of a brick wall. Tissue from a biopsy specimen is like seeing those fragments of an intact wall instead of just the bricks.[15]

A doctor performs a colposcopy on a female patient.

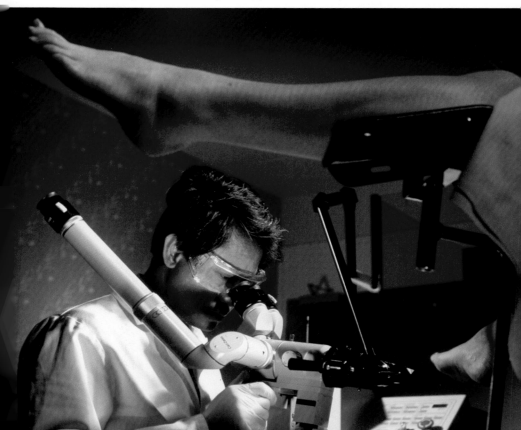

Thus, with a tissue sample from a biopsy, a pathologist can confirm the stage of HPV infection with a high degree of accuracy. At this point, in most cases the diagnosis is complete.

The HPV Genetic Test

However, although a biopsy is a reliable method to diagnose HPV, a precancerous lesion, or cervical cancer, it does have certain drawbacks. "The word 'biopsy' sends chills of horror through most [women]," Henderson points out. They "immediately conclude that they have cancer. Undergoing a biopsy can also be stressful and mildly painful. The procedure is slightly invasive and also costly."[16]

How Long Does an HPV Infection Last?

One question that patients diagnosed with HPV infections frequently ask their doctor is: How long will I remain contagious? Joel Palesfsky, a professor of medicine at the University of California–San Francisco, answers the question this way:

Many doctors take the position that HPV is most contagious in the months after you acquire your own HPV infection and develop dysplasia. Once you've had three or four normal Pap smears in a row, you're probably no longer infectious. However, since you may still have HPV even if you have a normal Pap smear, there's still a very small possibility that you could transmit HPV to a partner. If you're having regular sex with someone, it's very likely that they'll get HPV. . . . Once you have been diagnosed with HPV, my advice is to assume that you will always be infectious. This, of course, means you'll have to discuss HPV with a potential sexual partner.

Joel Palefsky, *HPV and Abnormal Pap Smears: What Your Doctor May Not Tell You.* New York: Warner, 2002, pp. 38–39.

As a result, some doctors are coming to rely on a relatively new procedure that can be classified as both a screening test and a diagnostic test for HPV. The new test, which the Food and Drug Administration (FDA) approved for use in 2000, works differently than the Pap smear. It is called the HC2 High-risk HPV DNA Test, or the HPV Test for short. The letters DNA in the test's full title reveal that it is genetically based. DNA is a complex chemical that carries the blueprints for the makeup of all living things on Earth. And each kind of living thing has a recognizable DNA, or genetic, fingerprint that makes it unique from other organisms. This is true even for viruses. Thus, the HPV test is designed to recognize the genetic fingerprints of several HPV viruses.

Cell samples for the HPV Test are collected in the same manner as those for Pap smears. A doctor scrapes some cells from the cervix onto a slide. But instead of examining the cells under a microscope, the lab technicians analyze them to determine their genetic contents. If any of the cells in the sample are infected with HPV, the genetic fingerprint of HPV will show up in the analysis. The test has at least one advantage over the traditional Pap smear. Namely, the genetic test can identify infected cells before they have developed enough dysplasia to be visible to technicians examining a Pap smear.

There is presently some disagreement among physicians over the size of the role that the HPV Test should play in HPV screening and diagnosis. Some doctors think that the new test should and will steadily replace Pap smears. "HPV testing as the stand-alone primary screening technology represents the scientifically obvious next step,"[17] noted Spanish physician F. Xavier Bosch stated in August 2006. But many of Bosch's colleagues insist that Pap smears should and will remain an essential tool and that the HPV Test should be used only as a supplement to the Pap test.

HPV in Men

So far, the emphasis has been on procedures for screening and diagnosing HPV in women. But what about men who carry or become infected by HPV? At present, no screening test for HPV

in men is widely accepted by the medical community. One reason is that it is considerably more difficult to collect a Pap-smear-like sample from the penis than it is from the vagina. (Most of the skin of the penis is too dry.) Also, penile cancer is far less common than cervical cancer. So no massive medical effort has been mounted to develop a reliable HPV test for men. As Palefsky states, "HPV infection of the penis is not on the radar screen of most men, and neither is it on the radar screen of most doctors."[18] Palefsky goes on to say that this is unfortunate because men do get infected by HPV on a regular basis. Like women, men usually exhibit no outward symptoms and therefore are not aware that they have HPV. And even though the virus does not usually harm men, they can easily pass it on to one or more sexual partners.

Because no widespread HPV screening test for men exists, direct examination of the penis is usually the only means of determining whether a man is infected. Said examination can be done with a colposcope, using a vinegar solution, in the same way it is done on a woman. However, this sort of examination is performed on men fairly infrequently. Many doctors feel that it is not warranted because HPV does not pose a serious threat to most men.

Checking Males for HPV

But some other physicians, including Palefsky, disagree. They prefer to check the male partners of women already diagnosed with an HPV infection. In fact, medical authorities estimate that about half of these male partners will display HPV lesions on the penis, but only a few of such lesions will become precancerous or cancerous. Roughly 85 percent of these penile lesions appear on the skin on the head or shaft of the penis. So they are readily visible in a colposcope. The other 15 percent appear in the urethra, the thin tube inside the penis. To examine this area, a doctor uses a urethroscope, a much smaller version of the colposcope. Some doctors also look for lesions in the man's anal area.

Assuming that the doctor finds no lesions in a man's genital region, the patient usually does not need further screenings.

Computer artwork of human papillomavirus particles is displayed here. Both men and women can become infected with HPV, but currently there aren't any widely available screening tests for men.

Some doctors recommend that men who worry about getting infected later perform self-exams in the same manner that women examine their own breasts for lumps that might lead to breast cancer. "The analogy that I use here," Palesfsky says, "is that of a cruise missile. A cruise missile has in its electronic brain a detailed image of the terrain that it needs to pass over to reach its programmed target. If a man memorizes the terrain of his penis . . . if and when something new crops up, he's more likely to recognize it."[19]

If either the doctor or the patient finds a suspicious lesion or lump in the penile or anal area, the next step is a biopsy. A pathologist can then determine if dysplasia or cancer is

present. Fortunately for men, this outcome is rare. The American Cancer Society reports that penile and anal cancer each affect only about one in every hundred thousand men in the United States. The CDC also has good news for the male population in general. "For most men," the CDC states, "there would be no need to treat HPV, even if treatment were available, since it usually goes away on its own."[20] Thus, some very reliable screening tests for HPV exist for women. And though no such tests are presently available for men, on the whole men do not need them.

Treatment for HPV Infections

At present, no definitive cure exists for HPV infections. However, a few treatments, mainly surgical, are sometimes employed to remove the lesions that HPV can cause on and beneath the skin. Also, HPV-induced cervical cancer can sometimes be treated using surgery, and genital warts can often be treated with topical creams and other drugs, as well as surgery.

Another approach to treating HPV infections is the development of vaccines. Two preventive vaccines designed to fight the onset of HPV infections were recently released by leading American pharmaceutical companies. Medical researchers say that these vaccines hold a great deal of promise for reducing the incidence of HPV infections in the United States and eventually across the world. In addition, several research facilities are presently trying to develop a therapeutic vaccine. It will hopefully eradicate the HPV virus even after it has taken hold in the body and caused various levels of dysplasia.

Keeping HPV from Spreading

The fact that medical science has been working on both preventive and therapeutic vaccines illustrates that prevention and treatment usually go hand and hand in medical science. And the situation with HPV is no different. For example, when someone is diagnosed with an HPV infection, especially if it is

high grade (HSIL or severe dysplasia), he or she naturally begins a treatment regimen overseen by a doctor. Whatever the chosen path of treatment might be, the doctor always gives the patient the same basic speech. During the period of treatment, the doctor explains, it very important for the patient to avoid spreading the virus to others.

In most cases this means that it is best to avoid sexual contact with other people. However, as the CDC explains, main-

A happy young couple. Maintaining a monogamous relationship can reduce the risk of contracting HPV.

taining a strictly monogamous relationship can be an acceptable alternative:

> The surest way to eliminate risk for genital HPV infection is to refrain from any genital contact with another individual. For those who choose to be sexually active, a long-term, mutually monogamous relationship with an uninfected partner is the strategy most likely to prevent future genital HPV infections. However, it is difficult to determine whether a partner who has been sexually active in the past is currently infected. . . . Partners less likely to be infected include those who have had no or few prior sex partners.[21]

One reason that keeping the risk of catching HPV within a single relationship can work is that, in the worst-case scenario, only one other person can become infected. Also, statistically speaking, there is a high likelihood that the virus will go away on its own in one or both partners. If and when that happens, that particular version of HPV will probably not return. "When an HPV infection goes away," ASHA reports, "the immune system will remember that HPV type and keep a new infection of the same HPV type from occurring again." However, ASHA continues, "Because there are many different types of HPV, becoming immune to one HPV type may not protect you from getting HPV again if exposed to another HPV type."[22] At any given time, the body's immune system targets only the specific virus it has encountered, not all HPV viruses. Thus, the partner of a person who is carrying two different HPV viruses could become infected. But even if that partner's system rids itself of that one virus, he or she could still become infected. This is why abstaining from sex altogether is the only 100 percent sure way of avoiding the spread of HPV.

LEEP and Cone Biopsy

While a woman diagnosed with an HPV infection is being careful to avoid further spreading the virus, her treatment for the infection begins. In most cases of mild dysplasia (LSIL) of the cervix (the area of the body most commonly treated for HPV),

Treatments vs. a Cure

It is important to understand that eliminating an HPV lesion through some kind of surgical procedure is not the same as curing someone of HPV. Doctors point out that existing surgical treatments for HPV lesions remove only the lesions, which are sores, or patches of abnormal cells, caused by the virus. These procedures do not remove the HPV virus from the body. It usually lingers, at least for a while, in other parts of the body, perhaps in the vagina, rectal area, or somewhere else. The virus might well go away on its own after a while. But in some cases it remains, lying dormant, and can reassert itself in the form of new, highly infectious lesions at any time.

a majority of physicians recommend no immediate treatment. This is based on the hope, backed up by statistics, that the infection will go away on its own after a few months. However, under certain circumstances, some doctors will advocate some form of treatment for mild dysplasia. For instance, the patient might claim that she does not have time to participate in regular follow-up exams and tests. In such a situation the doctor might feel it is best to stay on the safe side and go ahead with treatment.

In such cases, the treatments advocated are usually the same as in cases of moderate or severe dysplasia. The two most common treatments are both surgical, though each uses a different approach. Today, the most often performed procedure for removing HPV lesions from the cervix (or less frequently some other area of the body) is the loop electro-surgical excision procedure, called LEEP for short. LEEP uses a thin wire attached to an electrical generator. When the doctor presses the electrified wire loop onto the cervix, the wire slices through the tissue, excising, or removing, the infected area. Palefsky describes the basic steps a patient undergoes when having the procedure:

You'll have your feet in the stirrups [as in a Pap test] and a speculum in place, and your doctor will use a colpo-scope to view the procedure. . . . You'll either be given a local or, more rarely, a general anesthetic. With a local, you'll remain awake during the procedure, while a general anesthetic will put you to sleep. . . . After the anesthesia takes effect, your doctor will pass the wire loop through the surface of your cervix. After the lesion is removed, he or she . . . will send the removed tissue to the lab to provide a more accurate assessment of the abnormal area, as well as to make sure that the entire lesion was removed.[23]

The second most common surgical treatment for HPV lesions is the cone biopsy, also known as cold knife conization (or cold knife cone incision). The term "cold knife" refers to the fact that it is performed with a surgical scalpel. This procedure is most often done in a hospital setting (usually "day surgery"), and the patient is almost always given a general anesthetic. Once the patient is unconscious, the doctor cuts into the cervix and removes a cone-shaped piece of tissue (hence the terms "cone biopsy," "cone incision," and "coniza-tion"). "It's like taking the core out of the center of an apple," Henderson points out. "The scalpel is used to cut deep around the lesion so as to remove all of it."[24]

The Preferred Method

Although a cone biopsy can effectively remove an HPV lesion, the procedure sometimes has drawbacks. In particular, there is a risk of permanently disfiguring the cervix. This problem is called cervical incompetence. "So much muscle is removed from the cervix," says Henderson, "that the cervix is left unable to do what it is supposed to do—serve as a cuff to keep the uterus closed so that the fetus remains inside and germs remain outside."[25] Thus, cervical incompetence brought on by a cone biopsy can make it difficult or even impossible for a female patient to become pregnant.

In contrast, the LEEP procedure usually does less damage to the cervix. LEEP also produces less bleeding and has a

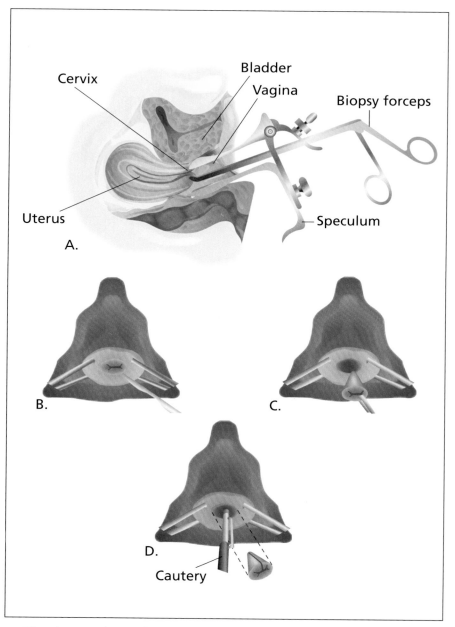

This diagram shows the steps involved in a cone biopsy. The patient lies on her back, and a speculum is inserted into the vagina (A). The cervix is visualized, and a cone-shaped piece of the cervix is removed (B and C). A cauterizing tool is used to stop any bleeding (D).

lower rate of postoperative infections. Still, the cone biopsy remains the preferred method in cases in which the doctor suspects that some parts of a precancerous lesion lie hidden deep in the cervical tissue. In such situations, removing a large amount of tissue may be the safer approach.

Laser Treatment and Cryotherapy

Two other surgical treatments for HPV lesions were used more often before LEEP became widely popular in the 1990s. However, both are still employed by some doctors, especially when a doctor feels a specific procedure will work very well in an individual situation. For example, the lesion might be easily visible and very small, and the doctor might want to minimize the amount of damage the surgery will do to surrounding healthy tissue.

In such a case, he or she may choose to use laser conization. A laser is a device that projects a highly focused beam of light. When properly calibrated and aimed, that beam can burn away abnormal or diseased tissue. One advantage of laser therapy is that the hot beam also seals blood vessels. This results in less bleeding than in most other surgical treatments. Also, little or no scarring occurs during the healing process that follows laser therapy.

Laser removal of HPV lesions usually takes place in a doctor's office with local anesthesia. As in LEEP and cone biopsies, the doctor uses a colposcope to view the cervix (or other area) during the procedure. He or she lines up the laser precisely (using a harmless beam of ordinary light), then turns on the laser and zaps the lesion.

In contrast, cryotherapy does cause considerable scarring during healing. And that is one of the reasons that doctors use cryotherapy far less often than either LEEP or laser treatment to deal with HPV lesions. The root word *cryo* means "cold" or "freezing," so cryotherapy destroys abnormal cells by freezing them. The doctor uses a probe that has been cooled to a very low temperature by exposure to liquid nitrogen. He or she holds the probe against the target area, which rapidly freezes into what Palefsky calls a "cervical ice ball."[26] After the operation

these frozen cells thaw, and then the cervix (or other area) steadily sheds them over the course of two or three months.

One advantage of cryotherapy is that it is highly effective for treating small patches of abnormal cells on the surface of the cervix. It is also relatively inexpensive and can be performed in a doctor's office. The procedure has several disadvantages, however. In addition to the scarring it causes post-op, cryotherapy has a fairly high failure rate in treating moderate and severe dysplasia. Also, the damage it does to the tissues often makes later Pap smears harder to interpret.

The New HPV Vaccines

Both patients infected with HPV and their doctors would quite naturally prefer not to have to resort to surgery to treat HPV infections. It would be much more desirable to be able to turn to less invasive treatments having few or no risks or potentially serious side effects. And indeed, a great deal of research is presently under way to develop such treatments.

Most of this research centers around HPV vaccines. Vaccines are substances that, when introduced into the body, stimulate the immune system to make antibodies. The antibodies are cells that attack a particular foreign intruder, including germs associated with various diseases. Thus, in theory, an HPV vaccine will prompt the immune system to attack one or more strains of the HPV virus and thereby keep the body safe from further infections by these strains.

After years of research and experiments, the Merck pharmaceutical company introduced an HPV vaccine in 2006. Called Gardasil, it was licensed by the FDA that same year. In 2007 another big drug company, GlaxoSmithKline, introduced a similar vaccine called Cervarix. These vaccines are made from proteins from the outer coat of certain HPV viruses. By themselves, the proteins are not complete viruses and therefore are not infectious and cannot cause disease. However, when the proteins enter the body during a vaccination, the immune system treats them as if they are complete viruses and attacks them. In the process, the body creates an immunity to these viruses.

The new HPV vaccines are designed to target HPV 16 and 18, which together cause some 70 percent of reported cases of cervical cancer. In addition, Gardasil protects against HPV 6 and 11, which cause about 90 percent of all cases of genital warts. These figures are impressive and heartening for HPV sufferers. But it must be kept in mind that the vaccines do not protect against the many other strains of HPV. Research is ongoing to develop vaccines that hopefully will do just that. Still, for the four HPV types targeted, the vaccines have proven almost 100 percent effective. Moreover, they have displayed no serious side effects in the more than eleven thousand women who received them in preliminary trials.

A vial containing one dose of Gardasil.

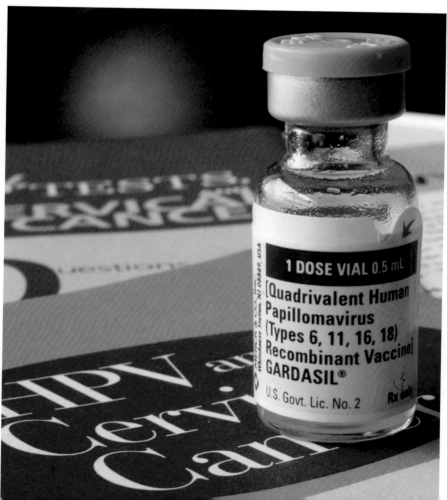

Who Should Get the Vaccines?

Strict guidelines determine how the new vaccines are given and who receives them. The vaccines are administered in three separate shots over a six-month period. The second shot is given two months after the first and the third shot six months after the first.

As for the target population, the Food and Drug Administration (FDA) has licensed Gardasil specifically for girls and women aged nine to twenty-six. The vaccine is most recommended for girls aged eleven to twelve because studies have determined that they can benefit most. The CDC explains why:

> Ideally, females should get the vaccine before they are sexually active. This is because the vaccine is most effec-

A young woman receives an injection of Gardasil.

tive in girls/women who have not yet acquired any of the four HPV types covered by the vaccine. Girls/women who have not been infected with any of those four HPV types will get the full benefits of the vaccine.[27]

Nevertheless, older, sexually active women will also benefit from the vaccines, though not as much because they have already been exposed to several HPV virus strains. Tests are now under way on women older than twenty-six. Depending on the results, the FDA may or may not license the vaccines for women in that age group. More research will also be needed before the vaccines can be recommended for pregnant women.

Drawbacks of the Vaccines

Although the new vaccines are a major step forward in the fight against HPV infections and HPV-related diseases, they do have certain drawbacks. First, because they do not protect against all HPV virus strains, women who are vaccinated can still acquire HPV infections. They must, therefore, continue to have regular Pap smears.

Second, the new vaccines are essentially preventative. This means that they can protect against contracting some strains of HPV, but they cannot destroy existing HPV lesions, whether mild, precancerous, or cancerous. (Therapeutic vaccines that will hopefully cure existing HPV infections are now under development.)

Another drawback of the new vaccines is that they are expensive. In fact, Gardasil is the most expensive vaccine ever developed. It costs $120 per dose, or $360 for the complete series of shots. Some insurance companies have indicated that they will pay for the shots, but others say they will not. In the United States free vaccinations are still and will continue to be available for some people. Some federal health programs give free vaccinations, for instance. One of these programs, Vaccines for Children (VFC), offers free injections of various vaccines to children from uninsured families, as well as all Native American children. Also, many hospitals and private clinics offer free vaccination programs. Several other developed

Can Boys Benefit from the Vaccine?

One question that doctors and other medical personnel who deal with STDs get asked on a regular basis is: Can the new HPV vaccine, Gardasil, be used for boys as well as girls? After all, males carry and contract the virus, too, and they can pass it on to females during sex or some other form of skin-to-skin contact. The CDC currently provides the following answer to the question:

We do not yet know if the vaccine is effective in boys or men. It is possible that vaccinating males will have health benefits for them by preventing genital warts and rare cancers, such as penile and anal cancer. It is also possible that vaccinating boys/men will have indirect health benefits for girls/women. Studies are now being done to find out if the vaccine works to prevent HPV infection and disease in males. When more information is available, this vaccine may be licensed and recommended for boys/men as well.

Centers for Disease Control and Prevention, "HPV Vaccine Questions and Answers." www.cdc.gov/STD/HPV/STDFact-HPV-vaccine.htm#hpvvac1.

countries, including the United Kingdom, France, Canada, and Australia, similarly offer some free vaccination programs.

The situation is quite different for women in poorer, third-world countries, however. There, both Pap smears and HPV vaccines are far beyond the financial means of most of the population. Fortunately, though, the Bill and Melinda Gates Foundation recently promised to fund HPV vaccination programs in a number of developing countries. As of February 2007, the foundation had committed $27.8 million to this effort.

An Ongoing Controversy

High prices and limited availability for poor people are not the only controversial aspects of the new HPV vaccines. A number

of religious and/or conservative organizations in the United States have voiced concerns about the vaccines. The main worry voiced so far is that removing much of the risk of contracting HPV might cause an increase in sexual activity among teens. According to this view, many young people refrain from having sex because they fear catching STDs, including HPV. And making the vaccines available to children will encourage them to have sex.

The Bill and Melinda (pictured here) Gates Foundation has pledged to fund HPV vaccination programs in developing countries.

Many medical experts and lawmakers disagree with this view. Late in 2005, with Gardasil about to be licensed, 103 members of the U.S. House of Representatives wrote to the CDC (which advises the FDA on medical matters), urging that there be no delays in authorizing use of the vaccine. The letter stated in part:

> Certain activists and organizations are mounting a campaign to prevent this vaccine from becoming widely available. They cite the possibility that, by preventing a horrible disease, and more than 3,700 deaths a year, this vaccine could remove an obstacle to teenage sex. . . . In contrast to the strong scientific evidence supporting the effectiveness of the . . . vaccine, there is no scientific evidence to support the fear that its use will promote sexual activity.[28]

Voluntary or Mandatory?

In fairness to the conservative organizations in question, most do not advocate banning or suppressing the HPV vaccines. Rather, their main concern is government mandates, or requirements, that children be vaccinated. Instead, they say, such vaccinations should be voluntary. As Peter Sprigg, vice president of the conservative Family Research Council, puts it:

> Pro-family groups are united in believing that parents should decide what is best for their children. We oppose any effort by states to make Gardasil mandatory (for example, making it a requirement for school attendance). If use of the vaccine becomes part of the recommended standard of care, and if the federal Vaccines for Children program pays for vaccination of those children whose families cannot afford it, then vaccination should become widespread without school mandates.[29]

This feared mandatory HPV vaccination program for young people became a reality on February 2, 2007. On that day Texas's Republican governor, Rick Perry, issued an executive order, bypassing the state legislature. As reported the next day by Liz Peterson of the *Dallas Morning News*:

Texas governor Rick Perry discusses his order to vaccinate all Texas schoolgirls against HPV.

Beginning in September 2008, [Texas school] girls entering the sixth grade—meaning, generally, girls ages 11 and 12—will have to receive Gardasil, Merck & Co.'s new vaccine against strains of the human papilloma virus, or HPV. Perry also directed state health authorities to make the vaccine available free to girls 9 to 18 who are uninsured or whose insurance does not cover vaccines. . . . Perry, a conservative Christian . . . said the cervical cancer vaccine is no different from the one that protects children against polio.[30]

Although Texas is the first state to make HPV vaccinations mandatory, it is not likely to be the last. The Michigan senate tried to pass a bill ordering the vaccination of young girls in September 2006. And although the bill failed to pass, supporters have reintroduced it. Moreover, numerous other states are expected to follow Texas's lead and enact similar programs in the near future. Meanwhile, a number of local and national groups opposed to such programs have promised to try to block them.

The controversy over administering the HPV vaccines to children demonstrates that strictly medical considerations are not the only factors that determine public health policy. And whatever vaccines and other treatments for HPV are introduced in the years to come, not everyone will approve of and use them. As in the case of the range of available surgical treatments, individual patients, or their parents, will make choices based on their personal needs and beliefs.

Diagnosing and Treating Genital Warts

While some strains of HPV cause lesions to develop in the genital area or elsewhere on the body, other strains can cause warts. Warts can appear practically anywhere on a person's body. And they are always unsightly, uncomfortable, and should, when a doctor advises it, be removed. However, they are most worrisome and unwanted when they infect the genital areas of women or men. "Although genital warts aren't fatal," Palefsky points out, "they cause a lot of misery. They can burn, itch, or bleed. They look unsightly and they're embarrassing. They also cost a lot of money—our health care system pays hundreds of millions of dollars each year to get rid of them."[31] The medical name for genital warts is *condyloma acuminata*, but doctors usually refer to the condition either as condyloma or genital warts.

Ordinary Warts

Ordinary warts are the nongenital kind that can appear on almost any part of the body. When someone gets them on the soles of the feet, they are called plantar warts. Those that grow on the face and legs are often called flat warts. Most ordinary warts are small, grainy or rough, and can be white, pink, or tan in color. They are almost always painless and are not cancerous or otherwise dangerous. These kinds of warts can spread

not only through skin-to-skin contact, but also by touching an object recently touched by a person with warts.

Because ordinary warts are small and pose no danger to the body, in most cases doctors advise patients simply to leave them alone. However, some warts occasionally grow larger and require removal. Large plantar warts can make walking more difficult, for instance, and large warts on the face can be unsightly. One common removal method is to apply salicylic acid (marketed as Compound W) to the wart every day for sev-

A young boy applies medicine to his wart. Salicylic acid (also known as Compound W) is a common treatment for ordinary warts.

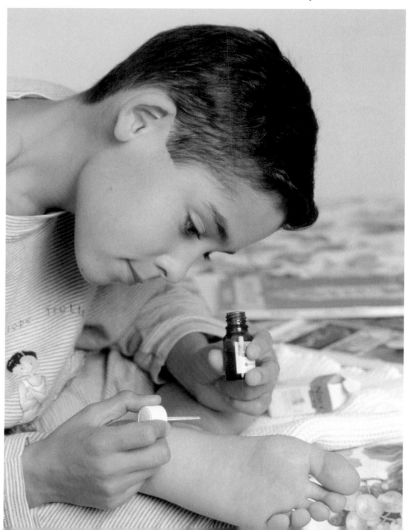

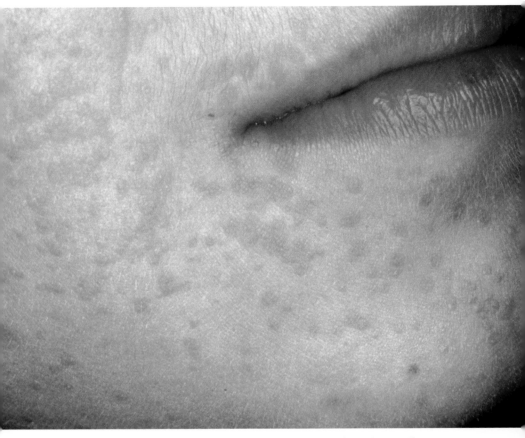

Ordinary warts that grow on the face are often referred to as flat warts.

eral weeks; little by little, this mild acid (which does not hurt the skin) breaks down the wart. Ordinary warts can also be removed by applying a little liquid nitrogen, which freezes them, or a small amount of a chemical called cantharidin, which dissolves them a little at a time.

Prevalence of Genital Warts

In contrast to ordinary warts, which may or may not need removal, everyone who contracts genital warts wants to get rid of them as quickly as possible. The exact prevalence of genital warts in society is unknown. This is largely because many people who contract these warts either do not realize it or are so

embarrassed that they do not report it. Thus, estimates vary somewhat for the total number of people infected. The lowest estimate suggests that about 1 million Americans have genital warts. That is 1 in every 272 people, or .37 percent of the population. Other medical authorities suggest that as many as 3 million people, or about 1 percent of the population, have genital warts. Whatever the real figure may be, it represents only those people who develop visible warts on the skin's surface. A much larger number of people, perhaps 4 percent of the population, may carry the HPV strains that cause genital warts but never actually develop any visible warts.

As for these HPV strains, the most common are HPV 6 and 11. They account for about 90 percent of all cases of genital

The Yuk Factor

Genital warts are widely seen as one of the more dreaded STDs, partly because people are naturally repulsed by the idea of having unsightly growths in their private parts. Medical experts sometimes call this the "yuk factor." Even doctors can experience the yuk factor when they first encounter genital warts. In his informative book about HPV, physician Gregory S. Henderson describes his own first experience in treating genital warts:

When I was a medical student, I was asked to examine a fifteen-year-old girl. . . . She was seeking treatment because she and her boyfriend could no longer have intercourse due to some problem in her genital area. When I examined the area, [I saw that] her vulva was covered by enormous cauliflower-like growths. The warts were so extensive that I couldn't even get a speculum into her vagina. I managed to mumble something about needing "another opinion" and hurried out of the room. I located [a more experienced doctor]. After she examined the girl, I received my first lecture on genital warts and HPV.

Gregory S. Henderson et al., *Women at Risk: The HPV Epidemic and Your Cervical Health.* New York: Penguin, 2002, pp. 97–98.

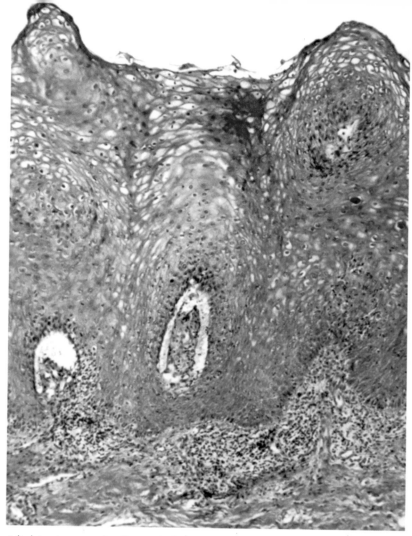

A light micrograph of a genital wart on the cervix. Lesions are seen at upper right, center, and center left. Spikes are formed at the surface of the wart (top right and top left).

warts. However, HPV 42, 43, 44, 51, 53, and 54 can also cause the condition. And on occasion, HPV 1, 2, and 4, which cause warts on the hands and feet, can be transferred to the genital region by touching one area and then the other.

Symptoms of Genital Warts

In fact, condyloma can appear anywhere in the genital region. That means that a woman can get the warts on her cervix, vagina, vulva, or anus. And a man can develop genital warts on

his penis, scrotum (the sack holding the testicles), or anus. Moreover, both men and women occasionally get these warts in the mouth or throat, a situation that arises when the virus spreads during oral sex. In general, condyloma is very infectious, and having any sort of sex with an infected person is risky.

However, that does not mean that every person exposed to genital warts will catch them. Some people acquire one or more of the wart-producing HPV viruses but never develop any tangible warts on the skin. The reason that some people merely carry these viruses and others develop warts is uncertain. But doctors are fairly sure that certain factors increase the risk of developing genital warts. For example, a person whose immune system is weakened is more likely to develop warts than someone whose immune system is strong. Other risk factors include cigarette smoking and poor hygiene. Studies suggest that both of these increase the likelihood that people carrying specific HPV strains will develop genital warts.

For whatever reasons people may develop condyloma, they do not always realize they have it. This is because in some situations the warts display few or no symptoms. Genital warts on the cervix, for instance, very rarely display any clear-cut symptoms. In contrast, warts on the vagina, vulva, penis, and some other areas sometimes display symptoms that can range from minor to very uncomfortable or even painful. These symptoms can include itching and burning sensations. There can also be watery discharges from the vagina. In a minority of cases, sufferers also report minor bleeding after having sexual intercourse.

Making a Diagnosis

These same symptoms can also be signs of other STDs or non-STD-related conditions. So it is important that someone who notices one or more of these symptoms does not try to diagnose her- or himself. A doctor or other specially trained health care professional is always the best person to make the diagnosis. "I felt these little bumps just outside my vagina [on her vulva]," recalls Lucy, a twenty-two-year-old student who was diagnosed with genital warts in 2005.

I knew right away there was something wrong because I had never noticed them before. I got a mirror and looked down there . . . and it really grossed me out, if you know what I mean. I called one of my girlfriends and asked her if she knew what to do. She was grossed out, too, and said she didn't know . . . that I should probably see a doctor. So I called and made an appointment, and now I'm really glad I did.[32]

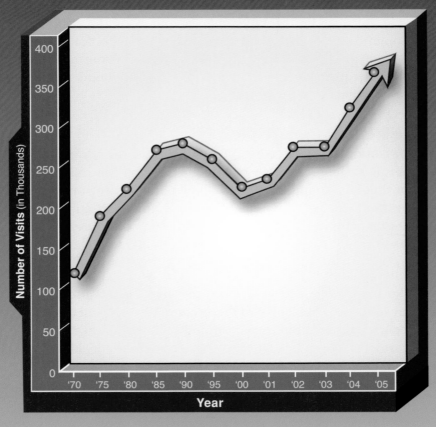

Visits to Physicians' Offices for Genital Warts, 1970–2005*

*Does not include visits for genital herpes.

Source: National Disease and Therapeutic Index (IMS Health).
www.cdc.gov/std/stats/tables/table42.htm.

As in the case of HPV lesions, to make the diagnosis the doctor most often uses a colposcope to examine the skin in one or more genital areas. Even under this device's magnification, the warts can be hard to see. Some look like very small raised bumps, not much bigger than so-called goose pimples. Others are flat and can range in color from brown to almost colorless; in the latter case, they can be almost invisible. In such cases, coating the area with a vinegar solution usually makes the warts stand out better.

In contrast, sometimes genital warts can be large, very unsightly bumps. They can also form thick clusters. When such a cluster of warts forms inside the urethra in the penis, it can be painful and the sufferer may have difficulty urinating. Similarly, a large cluster of genital warts in the vagina can be very uncomfortable and actually impede the act of sexual intercourse. Because both small and large bumps on the skin can be something else besides genital warts, if the doctor is still unsure after the visual exam, he or she can order a small biopsy. The tissue sample can then be examined under a microscope to make a definite diagnosis.

The Decision to Treat

After genital warts have been diagnosed, the doctor and patient must decide whether treatment is called for and, if so, what that treatment should be. Some patients are surprised when their doctors recommend a watch and wait approach rather than immediate treatment. But the fact is that very mild cases of condyloma frequently go away on their own, as often happens with the HPV virus in general. As Palefsky explains:

> The treatment of genital warts usually depends on the severity and persistence of the symptoms, the chances of recurrence, and your own desires as a patient. If only one wart exists, then you and your physician might decide to wait on treatment. Many genital warts regress on their own and never come back. . . . If the warts increase in size and number, though, you'll probably want to seek treatment sooner rather than later.[33]

It is important for doctors and patients to discuss treatment options after genital warts, as well as other types of warts, have been diagnosed.

If immediate treatment is called for, it can vary widely, depending on the individual patient as well as the individual doctor. "There are many different types of treatment for genital warts," Henderson says. And the choice of treatment depends "on the size and location of the wart [or warts], and how extensive the infection is. There is no single treatment . . . and different health-care practitioners seem to have their own preferences regarding which . . . medicine they start with and how they proceed."[34]

Patient-Applied Treatments

The many possible treatments for genital warts fall into two broad categories. The first is often referred to as "patient-applied" because the patient, following his or her doctor's

instructions, administers it, usually at home. One exception is pregnant women, whom doctors prefer to treat in a clinical setting, mainly because of concerns about possible complications for the developing fetus.

The most common patient-applied treatments for condyloma are topical creams and gels. (In medicine, the term *topical* refers to the skin and medicines applied to it.) Such products have some advantages. They are inexpensive when compared to other, more aggressive treatments, and they are very easy to apply. Also, to some degree they empower the patient, who may feel very positive about having a direct role in the treatment regimen.

The two leading topical medicines presently prescribed by doctors for genital warts are podofilox (sold as Condylox) and imiquimod (sold as Aldara). Podofilox is a gel that shrinks or destroys the warts, perhaps by stopping cell growth in them. The gel can be applied with the finger or, if the patient prefers, a cotton swab or Q-tip. As a rule, one applies it only to the largest, most persistent warts and it should not be used on an area larger than 1.5 square inches (10 sq. cm). The patient applies the gel twice a day for three days. If the warts grow smaller or go away, no more treatments may be necessary. If, however, the first treatment is ineffective, the patient can repeat it several times, taking four days off between each three-day regimen. Studies have shown that up to 88 percent of those who use podofilox respond well to the treatment. "Oh yes, I used it [podofilox]," says Lucy. "After a couple of weeks the warts were pretty much gone. To say I was relieved would be putting it mildly."[35]

Help from Interferons

Imiquimod, a cream that first became available in the 1990s, does not attack the warts directly, as podofilox does. Instead, imiquimod works by stimulating the tissues around the warts to produce interferons. Interferons are proteins the immune system manufactures to help fight infections. Like podofilox, imiquimod can be applied with the finger or a Q-tip. The normal regimen is to use it at bedtime three times a week until the

warts get smaller or disappear (but not longer than sixteen weeks). Roughly 50 percent of patients who used the cream say they are free of genital warts after about nine or ten weeks.

It is important to note that even when one of these topical medicines produces positive results, the warts may not be gone for good. They can recur, or come back, at any time and without warning. This is because the HPV strains that cause the warts are still in the person's body. "Therapies only treat the warts," Palefsky warns, "not HPV itself."[36] Medical authorities report that recurrence of the warts happens in nearly 50 percent of sufferers who use topical remedies.

Cryotherapy, Lasers, and Acids

The second general category of treatments for genital warts is doctor-administered (or provider-administered) therapy. Doctors have a wide range of choices at their disposal to deal with condyloma. Some are more complicated, time-consuming, and expensive than others, but all have a fairly good success rate in eliminating genital warts. However, none of these approaches can stop the warts from recurring unpredictably.

Among the more inexpensive and widely used doctor-administered treatments is cryotherapy. As in cryotherapy for HPV lesions, the procedure for warts employs an extremely cold probe, or in many cases liquid nitrogen itself. The doctor applies the probe or nitrogen directly to the target warts. The cold kills the cells in the warts and in a small amount of surrounding skin, and after a while these cells slough off (or shed). The patient usually has one session of cryotherapy in the doctor's office every one to two weeks until all of the warts are gone. One advantage of cryotherapy for condyloma (besides its reasonable cost) is that it rarely causes any scarring. Also, it is safe for pregnant women. Doctors report a nearly 90 percent success rate using this approach, with a recurrence rate of approximately 40 percent (somewhat better than that associated with topical creams).

Lasers can also be used to destroy genital warts. Most often, doctors employ a carbon dioxide laser, which vaporizes the warts. One disadvantage of the laser approach is that it is very

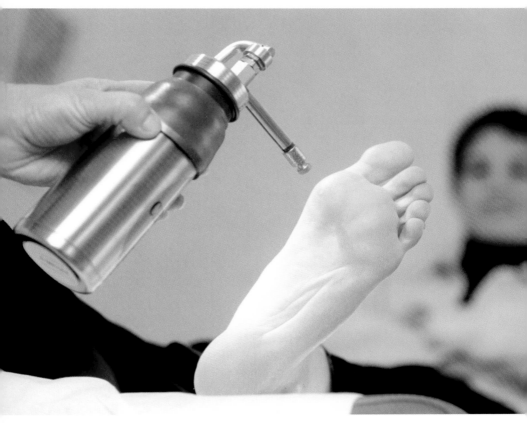

Cryotherapy is often used to treat warts. A cold probe or liquid
nitrogen is applied directly to the targeted area.

expensive, in part because the equipment involved is quite
costly. This treatment also requires a doctor who is specially
trained in the use of lasers. However, not every town is fortunate enough to have such an individual. Some physicians view
laser vaporization as a procedure of choice in certain situations. For example, it works exceptionally well in cases involv-
ing extensive clusters of warts. The laser also has a high
success rate in treating warts located in the urethra.

Another common doctor-administered treatment for genital
warts utilizes trichloroacetic acid, or TCA. Also, some doctors
use bichloroacetic acid, or BCA. Like cryotherapy and laser
vaporization, acid treatments can be done in a doctor's office

or clinic. Vaginal, vulvar, penile, urethral, and anal warts can all be treated successfully with this approach. The physician applies a small amount of the acid directly to one or more of the warts. After the acid dries, a white, frosty-looking residue appears on the warts, a sign that the acid has destroyed part of the wart. Patients often report a feeling of heat or occasionally mild pain during the procedure. The usual regimen is to repeat the acid therapy once a week for up to six weeks, after which, if the warts persist, the doctor will usually advise trying a different approach. TCA treatments have a success rate of about 80 percent, with a recurrence rate of about 36 percent.

Other Treatments

Topical remedies, particularly podofilox and imiquimod, and doctor-administered cryotherapy, laser, and acid procedures are usually the first line of defense against genital warts. And all of these can be effective in providing relief. However, none of these approaches is 100 percent effective. Moreover, no matter which of them is used, the warts can grow back later.

When condyloma does recur, doctors have a second line of defense at their disposal. It consists of a number of surgical and topical treatments that, like those in the first lines of defense, can be highly effective in some patients. Once again, different doctors prefer different treatments over others. And there is no standard approach or series of approaches.

Of these alternative treatments, surgical incision, or cutting away the wart or warts, is sometimes employed. This approach has two advantages. First, it can be performed in a doctor's office under local anesthetic. Second, when performed by a skilled physician, it requires only one visit, since the scalpel or sharp scissors he or she uses usually remove the warts entirely. A disadvantage of surgical incision is that, by definition, it does involve cutting. And some people are squeamish about the idea of applying a blade to their genital area unless their lives are at stake. Joe, who had anal warts in 2004, recalls: "I said no [to surgical incision] when my doctor listed the options. I mean, sure, if I had cancer down there it might be a different story. . . . I told him: if there's a less drastic way to do it, I'm there!"[37] Joe

ended up having his warts removed by cryotherapy. Another potential disadvantage of cutting away genital warts is that when a large cluster of warts is removed this way, the chance of recurrence is fairly high.

Another surgical procedure for treating condyloma is electrodessication (sometimes called electrosurgery). It is almost always employed only in cases in which one or more other treatments were tried first and did not work. This approach is similar to LEEP, used more often to treat HPV lesions, and uses similar equipment. Like surgical incision, electrodessication has the advantage of removing all the warts at once. However, the equipment needed is fairly expensive. Also, many doctors feel that laser vaporization works better because it produces less scarring. The warts tend to recur in 20 to 30 percent of patients who have electrosurgery.

Using Toxic Substances

Three other treatments sometimes used to treat genital warts employ toxic substances that either poison the warts or stimulate the immune system to destroy them. The substances involved are similar to those in the topical creams applied by patients. The difference is that a doctor applies more concentrated forms of these substances, usually as a last resort when other treatments have been ineffective.

Podophyllin resin, for example, is the active ingredient in podofilox, which many patients apply to their own warts. The doctor carefully applies a concentrated form of the resin directly to the patient's warts in each of several sessions. Because the resin is quite toxic, the doctor is careful not to get any of it on exposed healthy skin. Use of the resin was once more common and has declined in recent years as increasing numbers of physicians have come to prefer acid, liquid nitrogen, or laser treatments.

Another toxic substance, a cream called 5-fluorouracil, is also applied by a doctor directly to genital warts. It is usually employed to treat vaginal or vulvar warts. As in the case of podophyllin resin, the use of 5-fluorouracil cream has declined somewhat in recent years in favor of other treatments.

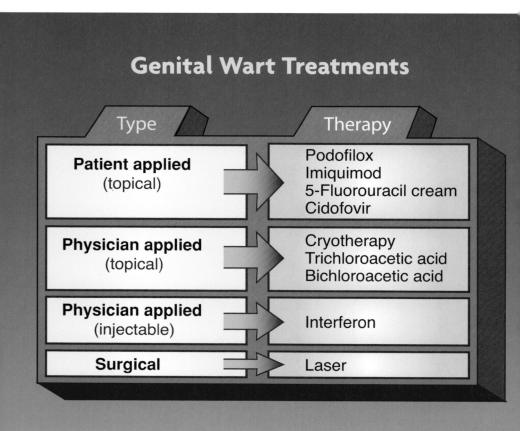

Genital Wart Treatments

Type	Therapy
Patient applied (topical)	Podofilox Imiquimod 5-Fluorouracil cream Cidofovir
Physician applied (topical)	Cryotherapy Trichloroacetic acid Bichloroacetic acid
Physician applied (injectable)	Interferon
Surgical	Laser

Perhaps the least often used treatment for genital warts is interferon therapy. Its principle is the same as that utilized by imiquimod topical cream, namely to stimulate the immune system to attack the warts. The difference is that interferon therapy takes place in a doctor's office and involves injecting pure interferon (a liquid made from bacterial cultures) into the patient. The doctor usually makes the injection at the base of each wart. Palesfsky explains why this approach is used less often than others: "It's expensive, inconvenient, requires many office visits, and is associated with a high rate of recurrence and adverse effects. Any benefits from interferon therapy can usually be obtained through more convenient, safer, less expensive routes."[38]

Preventing the Spread of Genital Warts

The American Social Health Association (ASHA) advises the following ways to reduce the risk of spreading and catching genital warts:

1. Not having sex with anyone.

2. Having sex only with one partner who has sex only with you. People who have many sex partners are at higher risk of getting other STDs.

3. If someone has visible symptoms of genital warts, he or she should not have sexual activity until the warts are removed.

4. Condoms, used the right way from start to finish each time of having sex may help provide protection, but only for the skin that is covered by the condom. Condoms do not cover all genital skin, so they do not protect 100 percent.

5. Spermicidal foams, creams, jellies (and condoms coated with spermicide) are not proven to be effective in preventing HPV and may cause microscopic abrasions that make it easier to contract STDs [including genital warts].

6. It is important for partners to understand the "entire picture" about HPV so that both people can make informed decisions based on facts.

American Social Health Association, "Genital Warts: Questions and Answers." www. ashastd.org/learn/learn_hpv_warts.cfm.

Thus, doctors use many and varied approaches to deal with genital warts. They and their patients agree that if there is anything good to say about these growths, it is that they are not life threatening, and one or more kinds of treatment will likely be effective. Unfortunately, however, the same often cannot be said of another common complication of HPV infections— cancer. Cancers caused by HPV have their own range of treatments. And when they fail, the results are tragic.

HPV and Cancer

The most dreaded and dangerous possible outcome of an HPV infection is the development of some form of cancer. Cervical cancer is the most common cancer type caused by the HPV virus, which is responsible for about 90 percent of all cases of cervical cancer. However, each year people around the world—both men and women—are diagnosed with other forms of cancer associated with HPV. These include, among others, vaginal cancer, cancer of the vulva, penile cancer (cancer of the penis), anal cancer, and oral cancer.

To appreciate the gravity of these diseases, how they spread, and how doctors attempt to treat them, it is important to understand what cancer is. This insidious disease is made up of groups of abnormal cells that appear inside the body and proceed to multiply. Most of the body's cells multiply by dividing in half from time to time, thereby creating new, healthy tissues while shedding older cells. For example, about once a month new bodily skin cells form and older ones fall away. In a manner that is still not well understood, the body tells these healthy cells that it is time to divide and also signals them when it is time to stop dividing.

This normal process of new cell creation is disrupted, however, in the case of cancer. Again for reasons that are somewhat uncertain, cells in one spot in the body do not receive the

"stop dividing" signal aimed at them. So these cells continue to divide and multiply. Over the course of days, weeks, and months, they form a cluster, called a tumor. The tumor often gets bigger and bigger until it begins to press on surrounding nerves, causing pain. If the abnormal cells multiply very slowly and are harmless to the body, the tumor is said to be benign, meaning "gentle." But if the abnormal cells continue to multiply and prove harmful to the body, the tumor is said to be malignant, meaning "harmful" or "cancerous." Cancerous tumors sometimes spread beyond the initial location of the tumor and invade other parts of the body, a process called metastasis. For example, cervical cancer caused by HPV can metastasize into cancer of the bladder, rectum, or even the lungs and liver.

Estimated New Cancer Cases, 2007

Type	Men	Women	Total
Cervical	N/A	11,150	11,150
Vaginal	N/A	2,140	2,140
Vulval	N/A	3,490	3,490
Penile	1,280	N/A	1,280
Anal	1,900	2,750	4,650
Oral cavity	24,180	10,180	34,360

Source: American Cancer Society. Cancer Facts & Figures 2007.
www.cancer.org/downloads/STT/CAFF2007PWSecured.pdf.

Vulvar Cancer

Vulvar cancer is cancer of the vulva, the area located just above the vagina and containing the labia (vaginal lips) and clitoris. The disease is fairly rare, with about 3,490 new cases and roughly 880 deaths in the United States in 2006. In the past, vulvar cancer affected almost exclusively women aged fifty or older. But the number of women younger than fifty diagnosed with the disease has been growing in recent years. Symptoms can include itching, a burning sensation, and/or small white bumps on the vulva. Pap smears are not reliable for detecting vulvar cancer, so regular pelvic exams by a doctor are the first line of defense against the disease. Typical treatments include surgical incision in the early stages and radiation therapy or chemotherapy in more advanced stages.

Diagnosing Cervical Cancer

Cervical cancer is not only the most common HPV-related cancer but also the second most common cancer that affects women worldwide (next to breast cancer). In the United States, however, cervical cancer is only the eighth most common cancer in women. Medical authorities believe this is due to the widespread use of Pap smears in American society. Pap tests alert numerous patients and doctors to the presence of severe dysplasia before it becomes cancerous. Nevertheless, the incidence of cervical cancer in the United States is still worrisome and tragic. An estimated 10,000 to 12,000 women contract the disease each year, and between 4,000 and 5,000 die from it.

Cervical cancer is most often caused by HPV 16 and 18, but others, including HPV 31, 33, 42, 42, and 58, can also cause it. Whichever virus strain is involved, its presence is frequently not the only factor in the development of the disease. Other factors that increase the risk of contracting cervical cancer include cigarette smoking, having many sexual partners, having

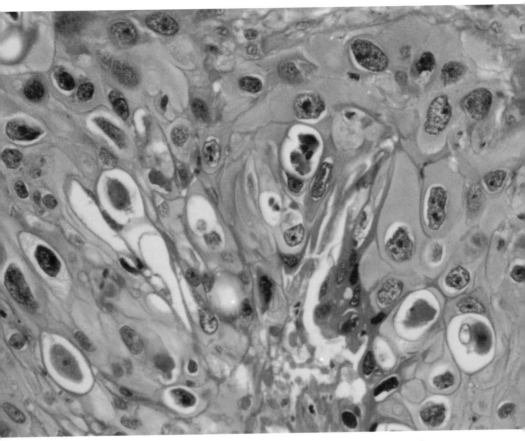

A light micrograph shows the presence of cervical cancer. This is the most common cancer caused by the HPV virus.

an existing HIV infection, poor diet, use of oral contraceptives, and multiple pregnancies.

Once HPV, aided by one or more of these other factors, has caused the development of a cancerous tumor, there are often no symptoms, at least in the early stages of the cancer. However, some women do experience symptoms. These can include vaginal bleeding, a pinkish-white discharge from the vagina, and/or a mass (lump) in the vagina that causes pain during sexual intercourse.

The range and severity of the symptoms depend to some degree on how the cancer spreads. As Rushing explains:

Cervical cancer generally spreads by invading nearby tissues in the area of the cervix where it first arose. The tumor may first invade the adjacent vagina and uterus and then later, if unchecked, spread to tissues outside the uterus, such as the bladder and rectum, which is the end portion of your colon. Advanced cervical cancers are notorious for blocking the ureters, the tubes that connect your kidneys to your bladder, which can cause urine to back up into the kidney and later damage it. . . . The greatest problems occur when cervical cancers invade blood and lymph vessels. This allows the cancer to spread more widely.[39]

The medical community has developed a list of typical stages to describe how cervical cancer spreads through the body. Categorizing the disease this way aids doctors trying to diagnose it and determine its extent. In general terms, stage 1 denotes those tumors confined to the uterus, most often the cervix itself and perhaps some surrounding tissues. In stage 2 the cancer has spread somewhat beyond the uterus. Stage 3 describes cases in which the cancer extends as far as the lower third of the vagina. And in stage 4 the cervical cancer has progressed to the bladder, rectum, and/or beyond.

To determine which of these stages of cervical cancer exists in a patient, a doctor goes through many of the same steps he or she would to diagnose HPV lesions. Close inspection of the cervix with a colposcope occurs. And this is often followed by a biopsy, after which a pathologist examines the excised tissue and looks for cancerous cells. In cases in which the cancer appears to be quite advanced, other diagnostic tests may be called for. For example, the doctor may x-ray the lungs or other parts of the body to see if the cancer has metastasized.

Surgical Treatments for Cervical Cancer

Treatments for cervical cancer usually vary according to its stage, or the extent to which it has spread. In mild stage 1 cases, for instance, in which the tumor is small and very localized, simple surgical excision (a cone biopsy) may be all that is required. The doctor cuts away the abnormal tissue plus, for

safety, some of the normal tissue surrounding it. Follow-up includes continued Pap smears and frequent checkups in the
doctor's office to be sure that the cancer has not returned.

In many cases, however, the cancer has spread too far for a
local surgical excision to be successful. The next step, assuming that the cancer has not spread beyond the cervix, is a radi-
cal trachelectomy, meaning removal of the entire cervix. This
procedure is almost always performed on younger women,
under the age of forty. It has the benefit of allowing many cervical cancer survivors to retain their uterus, which means that
they have a chance to become pregnant later.

This is unfortunately not the case with women whose cervical cancer has spread beyond the cervix. In such cases, the
doctor most often advises a hysterectomy. In this major operation, the cervix, uterus, and fallopian tubes (through which
eggs from the ovaries reach the uterus) are all removed, so
pregnancy is no longer an option. In hysterectomies done on
women over age forty, the ovaries are frequently removed, too.
And when they deem it necessary, doctors also remove the
lymph nodes surrounding the area. "Although it may seem like
a drastic measure," Palefsky notes,

> the alternatives are usually deemed so much less attrac-
> tive that [a] hysterectomy is preferable. The primary argu-
> ment against having a hysterectomy is that it removes the
> possibility of pregnancy, but the alternatives—radiation
> and chemotherapy—can also have long-term fertility
> problems.[40]

Other Treatments for Cervical Cancer

Of these alternative treatments, radiation therapy is often used
in cases in which, for one reason or another, women cannot
undergo conventional surgery. Or a doctor may decide that to
be safe, conventional surgery should be followed up by radiation therapy. The radiation kills the cancer cells, or prevents
them from further dividing, or both.

Two general kinds of radiation therapy are used to treat cervical cancer. Of these, internal radiation therapy is somewhat

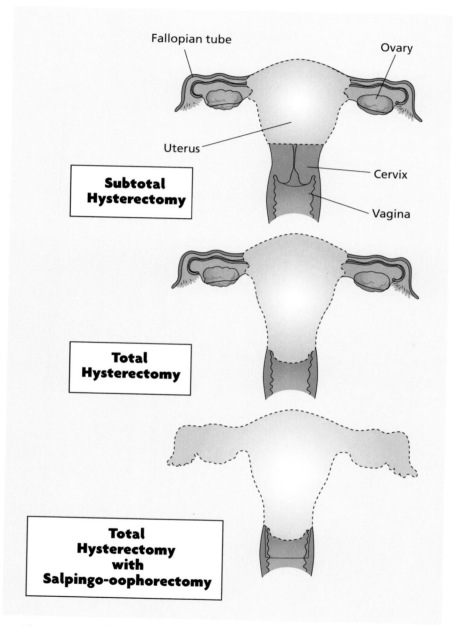

This diagram illustrates the three types of hysterectomies: subtotal (removal of the uterus), total (removal of the uterus and cervix), and total with salpingo-oophorectomy (removal of the female reproductive system).

less common. While the patient is under either local or general anesthetic, a thin tube is inserted into her vagina and placed up against the affected region of the cervix. Inside the tube is a radioactive material, most often cesium, iodine, iridium, or phosphorus, that unleashes deadly rays onto the cancerous cells. This usually occurs in a hospital setting to ensure complete control of the radioactive material, which is hazardous.

The other kind of radiation therapy used to combat cervical cancer is external, meaning the radiation source is outside the

Radiation therapy is often used to treat cervical cancer. A machine emits X-rays directly at the cancer. Shown here is a woman undergoing radiation treatment for skin cancer.

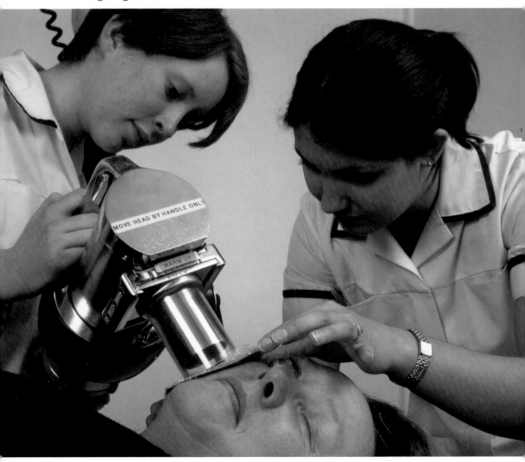

body. A machine emits highly concentrated X-rays, electron beams, or cobalt-60 gamma rays. These bursts of radiation are aimed directly at the cancer for as little as less than a minute to as long as five minutes, depending on the individual case. Several sessions of radiation therapy over the course of a few weeks or more are usually necessary.

Following these treatments, women often feel tired. Also, they may experience patches of dry skin in the treated area, which may also feel itchy or hard. Minor swelling in and around the target area can also occur. Such side effects are almost always temporary and steadily go away after the final treatment session.

Chemotherapy, which uses potent drugs (including 5-flourouracil) to fight the cancer, is sometimes used in conjunction with radiation therapy. The drugs are mostly either injected with a needle, administered through an IV tube, or taken orally. When they are used together, chemotherapy and radiation therapy can be considerably more effective than when only one is used. However, chemotherapy has a number of very unpleasant side effects. These can include nausea, vomiting, kidney damage, hair loss, and/or damage to the immune system. So both doctor and patient must carefully weigh the benefits and drawbacks of choosing chemotherapy, whether it is used alone or along with radiation therapy.

A newer, more preventive treatment that promises to reduce the incidence of cervical cancer consists of the recently released HPV vaccines. Both Gardasil and Cervarix are designed to target HPV 16 and 18. These strains cause not only a hefty number of HPV infections but also the majority of cervical cancers. Medical authorities are therefore hopeful that in the coming years increased use of these and other similar vaccines will result in fewer cases of cervical cancer.

Vaginal Cancer

Fortunately, vaginal cancer is less widespread than cervical cancer. The National Cancer Institute estimates that there were about 2,420 new cases of vaginal cancer in the United States in 2006 and that about 820 women died of the disease

A woman receives chemotherapy treatment.

that year. Not all vaginal cancers are associated with HPV, nor do all cases of vaginal cancer arise from vaginal dysplasia. However, roughly 85 percent of vaginal cancers begin growing in the squamous cells of the vagina. And most of these tumors are linked to some of the same HPV strains associated with cervical cancer.

The treatments for these sorts of vaginal cancers are similar to some of those used to deal with severe dysplasia and cervical cancer. If the doctor finds a lesion and determines it is precancerous, he or she can surgically remove it using LEEP. If the diagnosis is more serious—actual vaginal cancer—early stages are usually treated either with surgical removal or radiation therapy. More advanced stages of the disease are generally treated with radiation.

If the radiation therapy fails to destroy all the cancer, more extreme measures may be necessary to save the patient's life. Partial removal of the vagina is one of these measures. The next step, if the doctor deems it appropriate, is complete removal of the vagina (a vaginectomy). If the cancer has spread beyond the vagina, a hysterectomy is usually performed. And in the most extreme cases, in which the cancer keeps coming back, it might be necessary to resort to a pelvic exenteration. According to one medical authority:

> Pelvic exenteration is considered a "last resort" measure, and is usually reserved for recurrent cases. Exenteration removes the vagina, cervix, uterus, rectum, lower colon, or bladder, depending on where the cancer has spread. Reconstruction [using plastic surgery] of the vagina, bladder, and colon are usually necessary.[41]

Penile Cancer

Penile cancer is another fairly rare cancer that is often (though not always) associated with the HPV virus. The American Cancer Society and other medical authorities estimate that penile cancer affects about one in 100,000 men per year in the United States. In hard numbers, approximately 1,530 American men had penile cancer in 2006 and about 280 of these men died.

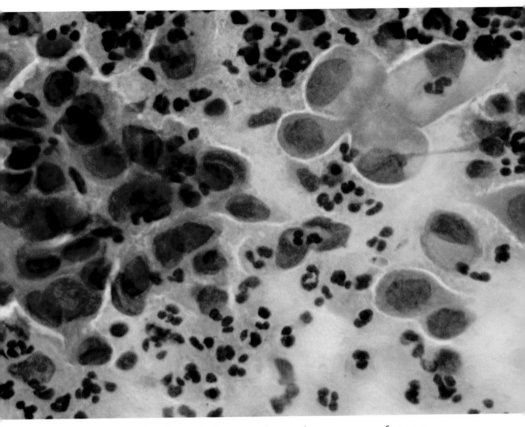

A light micrograph of a vaginal smear shows the presence of cancer cells. Vaginal cancer is less common than cervical cancer.

Higher rates of the disease are found in many other parts of the world. This is especially true in poorer countries where proper personal hygiene can be less prevalent and where fewer doctors and medical facilities exist to aid sufferers. Studies have shown that uncircumcised men have a higher risk of contracting HPV infections, penile dysplasia, and penile cancer. This is because these problems most often occur under the foreskin, where poor hygiene increases their likelihood.

When penile cancer is diagnosed and caught in its early stages, a small biopsy (sometimes called microsurgery) may effect a cure. If the man is uncircumcised, the doctor may remove the foreskin at the same time. This will lower the risk of

recurrence. If the cancer is more advanced, radiation therapy and chemotherapy are frequent options. But in extreme cases, when there is no other choice, a penectomy (removal of the penis), is performed. Plastic surgery can reconstruct the penis afterward, allowing the man to urinate normally.

Anal Cancer and Oral Cancer

Among the other cancer types associated with HPV are anal cancer and oral cancer. About 4,660 cases of anal cancer were diagnosed in the United States in 2006, among whom roughly 1,910 were men and 2,750 were women. Approximately 660 of these people died of the disease. Anal cancer is most often associated with HPV 16 and 18, the same two that cause a majority of cervical cancers. This means that a woman with cervical dysplasia or cervical cancer is at risk for anal cancer, too. The risk of anal cancer is also higher for people who engage in certain behaviors, notably smoking, having multiple sex partners, and engaging in anal intercourse. In gay men, the risk of contracting anal cancer is about seventeen times greater than in straight men.

The symptoms of anal cancer can be somewhat different than for most other cancers caused by HPV, although diagnosis and treatment are generally the same. The Abramson Cancer Center at the University of Pennsylvania provides this clearly stated overview of anal cancer symptoms:

> In about 50% of cases, the initial symptom of anal cancer is bleeding. Pain is somewhat less common, seen in about 30% of patients presenting with anal cancer; however, it can be quite severe. Occasionally, patients have the sensation of having a mass in the anus and can experience itching or anal discharge. Rarely, in advanced cases, anal cancers can disrupt the function of the anal muscles, resulting in loss of control of bowel movements. In general, these symptoms are vague and non-specific. As a result, in one-half to two-thirds of patients with anal cancer, a delay of up to 6 months occurs between the time when symptoms start and when a diagnosis is made.[42]

Prevention of Anal Cancer

The Abramson Cancer Center at the University of Pennsylvania offers the following advice about preventing the contraction of anal cancer:

Anal cancer is an uncommon cancer, and the risk of developing anal cancer is quite low. However, by avoiding the factors that are known to be related to anal cancer, the risk of developing anal cancer will become even lower. By far, the most important factor in developing anal cancer is infection with HPV. . . . Avoiding smoking and unsafe sexual practices can [also] reduce the risk of anal cancer. In patients who are known to have anal dysplasia, careful surveillance can result in early detection of anal cancer, and a higher rate of cure with treatment.

Abramson Cancer Center, University of Pennsylvania, "Anal Cancer: The Basics." www.oncolink.com/types/article.cfm?c=5&s=10&ss=776&id=9497.

Diagnosis of anal cancer is usually done in the standard manner—using colposcopy and biopsy. The most common treatment is radiation therapy using high-energy X-rays. The patient receives doses of radiation daily, Monday through Friday, for five to six weeks. Surgical removal, followed by a regimen of chemotherapy is also sometimes employed.

HPV-related oral cancer also poses a risk to people everywhere. About thirty thousand Americans get oral cancer each year and roughly eight thousand of them die. Numerous studies have confirmed that the majority of these cases are caused by tobacco and alcohol use. However, in the past few decades there has been an alarming increase in the number of oral cancers caused by HPV 16 and to a lesser extent other HPV types. These viruses may now account for as many as 15 to 25 percent of all oral cancer cases. Medical authorities say that most often the viruses spread from the genital region to the mouth during oral sex. Surgical excision, radiation therapy, and chemotherapy are all used to treat oral cancer.

Some Bad and Good News

Whether it is oral, anal, cervical, or another kind of cancer, or genital warts, or simple dysplasia, the adverse consequences of contracting HPV are many and diverse. The bad news is that these consequences are at the very least unpleasant and sometimes they can be lethal. Medical experts agree that the best way to avoid infection by HPV in general is to avoid certain risky behaviors. These include, among others, having unprotected sex, having multiple sex partners, smoking, practicing poor hygiene, and eating a poor diet (which weakens the immune system).

The good news is that many treatments are available for HPV-related dysplasia, precancers, cancers, and warts. The key, as in any disease or medical condition, is often early detection. That is why it is imperative for women to get regular Pap smears. If diagnosed in its early stages, almost any condition caused by HPV can be treated successfully. And new and promising treatments, including preventative and therapeutic vaccines, are presently under development.

Of course, avoiding risky behaviors is much easier for those who have a basic knowledge of HPV and its risks and consequences in the first place. In fact, only through education about HPV and other STDs can people avoid these diseases and move ever closer to eradicating them. In Palefsky's words:

> [When] you know the facts about HPV . . . you have real information you can use in your present and future. You can never go into the past and "un-get" HPV, but you have complete control of your own future. Learn as much as you can, use that information wisely, and take control![43]

Notes

Introduction: The STD Most People Never Heard Of

1. Gregory S. Henderson et al., *Women at Risk: The HPV Epidemic and Your Cervical Health*. New York: Penguin, 2002, p. 11.
2. Henderson, *Women at Risk*, p. 6.
3. Henderson, *Women at Risk*, p. 7.
4. Joel Palefsky, *HPV and Abnormal Pap Smears: What Your Doctor May Not Tell You*. New York: Warner, 2002, p. 4.

Chapter 1: Finding Reliable Facts About HPV

5. American Social Health Association, "HPV: Myths and Misconceptions." www.ashastd.org/hpv/hpv_learn_myths.cfm.
6. Karen, interview by the author, 2007.
7. American Social Health Association, "HPV: Myths and Misconceptions."
8. Henderson, *Women at Risk*, p. 40.
9. Mary, interview by the author, 2007.
10. Palefsky, *HPV and Abnormal Pap Smears*, p. 21.
11. Lynda Rushing et al., *Abnormal Pap Smears: What Every Woman Needs to Know*. Amherst, NY: Prometheus, 2001, p. 22.

Chapter 2: Screening for and Diagnosing HPV

12. Henderson, *Women at Risk*, p. 54.
13. Henderson, *Women at Risk*, p. 55.
14. National Cancer Institute, "The Pap Test: Questions and Answers." www.cancer.gov/cancertopics/factsheet/Detection/Pap-test.
15. Rushing, *Abnormal Pap Smears*, p. 81.

16. Henderson, *Women at Risk*, p. 76.

17. Quoted in Andrew Pollack, "Pap Test, a Mainstay Against Cervical Cancer, May Be Fading," *New York Times*, January 16, 2007. www.nytimes.com/2007/01/16/health/16pap.html?pagewanted=2&ei=5088&en=9e3e93d58f4dd2b9&ex=1326603600&partner=rssnyt&emc=rss.

18. Palefsky, *HPV and Abnormal Pap Smears*, p. 291.

19. Palefsky, *HPV and Abnormal Pap Smears*, p. 299.

20. Centers for Disease Control and Prevention, "HPV and Men." www.cdc. gov/STD/HPV/STDFact-HPV-and-men.htm.

Chapter 3: Treatment for HPV Infections

21. Centers for Disease Control and Prevention, "Genital HPV Infection." www.cdc.gov/std/HPV/STDFact-HPV.htm.

22. American Social Health Association, "HPV in Relationships." www.ashastd.org/hpv/hpv_learn_relationships.cfm.

23. Palefsky, *HPV and Abnormal Pap Smears*, pp. 134–35.

24. Henderson, *Women at Risk*, p. 82.

25. Henderson, *Women at Risk*, p. 83.

26. Palefsky, *HPV and Abnormal Pap Smears*, p. 139.

27. Centers for Disease Control, "HPV Vaccine Questions and Answers." www.cdc.gov/STD/HPV/STDFact-HPV-vaccine.htm#hpvvac1.

28. Quoted in Nancy Gibb, "Defusing the War over the 'Promiscuity' Vaccine," *Time*, June 21, 2006. www.time.com/time/nation/article/0,8599,1206813,00.html.

29. Peter Sprigg, "Pro Family, Pro Vaccine, but Keep It Voluntary," *Washington Post*, July 15, 2006. www.washingtonpost.com/wp-dyn/content/article/2006/07/14/AR2006071401532.html.

30. Liz Peterson, "Texas Governor Orders Anti-cancer Vaccine for School Girls," *Dallas Morning News*, February 3, 2007. www.dallasnews.com/sharedcontent/APStories/stories/D8N1TCI80.html.

Chapter 4: Diagnosing and Treating Genital Warts

31. Palefsky, *HPV and Abnormal Pap Smears*, p. 254.

32. Lucy, interview by the author, 2007.
33. Palefsky, *HPV and Abnormal Pap Smears*, p. 266.
34. Henderson, *Women at Risk*, p. 100.
35. Lucy, interview.
36. Palefsky, *HPV and Abnormal Pap Smears*, p. 261.
37. Joe, interview by the author, 2007.
38. Palefsky, *HPV and Abnormal Pap Smears*, p. 276.

Chapter 5: HPV and Cancer

39. Rushing, *Abnormal Pap Smears*, p. 119.
40. Palefsky, *HPV and Abnormal Pap Smears*, pp. 156–57.
41. Palefsky, *HPV and Abnormal Pap Smears*, p. 200.
42. Abramson Cancer Center, University of Pennsylvania, "Anal Cancer: The Basics." www.oncolink.com/types/article.cfm?c=5&s=10&ss=776&id=9497.
43. Palefsky, *HPV and Abnormal Pap Smears*, p. 339.

Glossary

basal cells: Cells located in the lower portion of bodily tissues; basal cells regularly divide, creating new cells.

biopsy: The surgical removal of a small amount of bodily tissue, either for diagnostic purposes or as treatment.

cervical cancer: Cancer of the cervix, the lower, narrow portion of the uterus, leading into the vagina.

chemotherapy: Medical treatment that uses potent drugs to fight cancer or another disease.

colposcope: A device equipped with a magnifying lens, used by doctors to examine the surface of the skin; the procedure in which a colposcope is used is called a colposcopy.

condyloma (short for *condyloma acuminata*): The medical name for genital warts.

cone biopsy (or cold knife conization, or cold knife cone incision): The surgical removal of a wedge-shaped piece of tissue from the cervix or another part of the body.

cryotherapy: A medical treatment that uses extreme cold to freeze and destroy abnormal or diseased bodily tissue.

cytotechnologist: A lab technician who specializes in reading Pap smears and other cell samples taken from patients.

diagnosis: A conclusive identification of a disease or other medical condition.

dysplasia: An area of abnormal cells.

electrodessication: A surgical procedure in which genital or other warts are burned away by an electrical current.

genitals: The reproductive organs and surrounding areas, including the vagina, vulva, cervix, penis, scrotum, and anus.

genital warts: HPV-related growths that develop in the genital area.

human papillomavirus (HPV): A series of more than a hundred viruses that can cause skin lesions, warts (including genital warts), and/or various forms of cancer.

imiquimod: A topical cream usually applied by patients to treat their genital warts.

laryngeal papillomatosis: HPV-related warts or other growths that form in the throat, specifically the larynx, or voice box.

laser conization (or vaporization): A medical procedure that uses a laser to burn away abnormal or diseased bodily tissue.

lesion: A sore or other abnormality, usually on the skin.

loop electrosurgical excision procedure (LEEP): A surgical procedure that uses a thin wire attached to an electrical generator to cut away diseased bodily tissue.

metastasis: The spread of cancer from its initial location to other parts of the body.

Pap smear (or Pap test): A preventive test that reveals the presence of an HPV infection.

pathologist: A doctor who is specially trained to recognize and identify various diseases by examining tissue samples.

pelvic exenteration: A complex surgery in which the vagina, cervix, uterus, rectum, and/or lower colon and bladder are removed.

penectomy: Removal of the penis.

podofilox: A topical cream usually applied by patients to treat their genital warts.

podophyllin resin: A topical medicine applied by a doctor to treat genital warts.

precancerous: Having the potential or likelihood to develop into cancer.

radiation therapy: Medical treatment that uses high-energy X-rays or other kinds of radiation to fight cancer.

screening test: A preventive medical test designed to look for signs of a disease or condition in a group of people who are at high risk of contracting the disease or condition.

speculum: A device that holds open the vagina during a medical exam or procedure.

squamous cells: Cells located in the outer portion of the skin.

trachelectomy: Removal of the cervix.

trichloroacetic acid (TCA): An acidic solution applied by a doctor to treat genital warts.

urethroscope: A smaller version of a colposcope, used for examining the urethra, the tube though which urine passes out of the body.

vaccine: A substance that stimulates the body's immune system to fight off invading disease germs.

vaginectomy: Removal of the vagina.

virus: A microscopic germ that invades and multiplies inside living cells.

Organizations to Contact

American Social Health Association (ASHA)
PO Box 13827
Research Triangle Park, NC 27709-3827
(800) 227-8922
Web site: www.ashastd.org

ASHA describes itself as a trusted, nonprofit organization that advocates on behalf of patients to help improve public health outcomes. The organization delivers accurate, medically reliable information about STDs. Public and college health clinics across the United States order ASHA's educational pamphlets and books to give to clients and students. Community-based organizations depend on ASHA, too, to help communicate about risk, transmission, prevention, testing, and treatment.

Centers for Disease Control and Prevention (CDC)
1600 Clifton Rd.
Atlanta, GA 30333
(800) 232-4636
Web site: www.cdc.gov

The mission of the CDC is to protect people's health and safety, provide reliable health information, and improve health through strong partnerships. The organization offers a wealth of information about sexually transmitted diseases, including HPV, in pamphlets available by mail and on its Web site.

National Cancer Institute (NCI)
Public Inquiries Office
6116 Executive Blvd., Room 3036A
Bethesda, MD 20892-8322
(800) 422-6237

Web site: www.cancer.gov

The National Cancer Institute coordinates the National Cancer Program, which conducts and supports research, training, health information dissemination, and other programs with respect to the cause, diagnosis, prevention, and treatment of cancer, rehabilitation from cancer, and the continuing care of cancer patients and the families of cancer patients. Its Web site contains extensive information about the human papillomavirus and its consequences.

National Cervical Cancer Coalition (NCCC)
7247 Hayvenhurst Ave., Suite A-7
Van Nuys, CA 91406
(818) 909-3849
Fax: (818) 780-8100
Web site: www.nccc-online.org

The NCCC is a grassroots nonprofit organization dedicated to serving women with or at risk for cervical cancer and HPV disease. The NCCC educates the public about cervical cancer and maintains a support system for women with the disease.

National Library of Medicine MedlinePlus
8600 Rockville Pike
Bethesda, MD 20894
(888) 346-3656 or (301) 594-5983
Web site: www.medlineplus.gov

MedlinePlus brings together authoritative information from the National Institutes of Health (NIH) and other government agencies and health-related organizations. MedlinePlus also has extensive information about drugs, an illustrated medical encyclopedia, interactive patient tutorials, and the latest health news.

For Further Reading

Books

Louise I. Gerdes, ed., *Sexually Transmitted Diseases*. San Diego: Greenhaven, 2003. A very useful collection of short articles by doctors and other experts who discuss the best-known STDs, including HPV.

Kristen Kemp, *Healthy Sexuality*. New York: Franklin Watts, 2004. Aimed at young readers, this book introduces the basic facts about sexuality, including STDs and their consequences.

Lynda Rushing et al., *Abnormal Pap Smears: What Every Woman Needs to Know*. Amherst, NY: Prometheus, 2001. A straightforward presentation of the facts about Pap smears and how they can help to diagnose HPV and other medical problems.

Deborah A. Stanley, ed., *Sexual Health Information for Teens*. Detroit: Omnigraphics, 2003. A large, detailed collection of information about sexually transmitted diseases and other topics relating to human sexuality.

Amy L. Sutton, ed., *Sexually Transmitted Diseases Sourcebook*. Detroit: Omnigraphics, 2006. A superior reference manual dealing with all known sexually transmitted diseases in considerable detail.

Samuel G. Woods, *Everything You Need to Know About Sexually Transmitted Diseases*. New York: Rosen, 2003. An easy-to-read synopsis of the principal STDs, including HPV.

Web Sites

Cervical Cancer (www.cancer.gov/cancertopics/types/cervical). The main National Cancer Institute Web page about cervical cancer. Contains numerous useful links to sites providing a wide range of information about the disease.

Genital HPV Infection—CDC Fact Sheet (www.cdc.gov/std/ HPV/STDFact-HPV.htm). An excellent general overview of the basic facts about HPV, including what it is, how it spreads, and how it can be treated.

Myths and Misconceptions About HPV (www.ashastd.org/ hpv/hpv_learn_myths.cfm). This informative article from the American Social Health Association cites the most common myths about HPV and gives the real facts.

Questions and Answers About Pap Smears (www.cancer. gov/cancertopics/factsheet/Detection/Pap-test). A fact-filled synopsis of Pap smears and their importance from the National Cancer Institute.

Index

American Cancer Society, 38

American Social Health
Association (ASHA), 13,
41, 70

Anal cancer, 38
incidence/symptoms of, 83
prevention of, 84

Bethesda Classification
System, 31

Bichloroacetic acid (BCA), 66

Bill and Melinda Gates
Foundation, 50

Biopsy, 32–34
cone, 43, 44
for genital warts, 62

Birth, 25

Bosch, F. Xavier, 35

Cancers
estimated new cases of, *72t*
in men, 36, 38
risk factors for, 23

See also specific types

Centers for Disease Control
and Prevention (CDC), 17,
48–49

Cervarix, 46

Cervical cancer, 71
annual incidence, 27, 73
chemotherapy for, 79
diagnosis of, 73
light micrograph of, *74*
radiation therapy for, 76,
78–79
screening test for, 28, 29
sites of metastasis of, 72
staging of, 75
surgical treatment of,
75–76
symptoms of, 74

Cervical incompetence, 43

Cold knife conization, 43, *44*

Colposcopy, 32, *33*

Condoms, as protection
against HPV, 16, 70

Picture Credits

About the Author

In addition to his numerous acclaimed volumes on ancient civilizations, historian Don Nardo has published several studies of modern scientific and medical discoveries and phenomena. Among these are *Germs*, *Atoms*, *Biological Warfare*, *Eating Disorders*, *Breast Cancer*, *Vaccines*, *Malnutrition*, and biographies of scientists Charles Darwin and Tycho Brahe. Mr. Nardo lives with his wife Christine in Massachusetts.

SAHARA WEST